No Clouds Tomorrow

CAROL E. CRAIN

WESTBOW
PRESS®
A DIVISION OF THOMAS NELSON
& ZONDERVAN

WestBow Press books may be ordered through booksellers or by contacting:

WestBow Press
A Division of Thomas Nelson & Zondervan
1663 Liberty Drive
Bloomington, IN 47403
www.westbowpress.com
844-714-3454

Scripture taken from the King James Version of the Bible.

ISBN: 978-1-6642-3084-2 (sc)
ISBN: 978-1-6642-3085-9 (hc)
ISBN: 978-1-6642-3086-6 (e)

Library of Congress Control Number: 2021907579

Print information available on the last page.

WestBow Press rev. date: 05/17/2021

This book is dedicated to the relatives
and friends of Carol E. Crain.

Contents

Foreword

I met Carol in an English class in 1968 when we were juniors at Bob Jones University, Greenville, South Carolina. She was an elementary education major from Eighty Four, Pennsylvania.

Betty Day, Carol's mother, separated from her second husband and moved with Carol from Pennsylvania to Greenville during the summer before Carol and I met. Carol worked part time as a Walgreens restaurant waitress and shared an apartment with her mother, a secretary. I was a Greenville County native, lived with my parents, and worked part time at a printing company.

Carol learned I was an art student, introduced herself, and asked if I would draw a dachshund similar to her deceased pet, Heidi. I created a dachshund watercolor and asked Carol for a date. She told me of living in "two rooms and a bath" apartments with her mother and spending lots of time with her maternal grandparents.

Carol and I graduated in 1969 and taught school in Greenville County. I volunteered for the draft after a year as a public high school art teacher. We married in August 1970, and I spent Christmas in Vietnam. I never saw combat and returned to Greenville before Christmas 1971.

Our children arrived: Janelle in 1973 and Suzanne in 1978. In 1988 we moved to North Carolina because I worked in carpet manufacturing. Carol taught elementary school. We moved back to the Greenville area one year before Carol died on January 11, 2019.

"I accepted Christ at a Bible school when I was four-and-a-half years old," Carol told me. While her father was in the US Army, she was born in Oakland, California. Her parents divorced before her second birthday. Carol absorbed scripture and self-help books. She wanted her students to succeed and, on her own time, desired to show others that self-worth and salvation are found in Christ.

Carol wrote poems and songs though she had not learned to read music. Melodies came to her, she said, as if she were listening to tunes on the radio. I found chords on my guitar to go with her songs.

Carol often wrote about dealing with painful memories. One year when we were young parents, we celebrated Father's Day, and Carol began thinking about her father, who she met only once in her life. *Where is my father?* she wondered. *He has never shown any interest in me. He has never met my husband and child.* With tears flowing, she pounded the table and said, "Lord, it hurts me."

She then sang lines that came to her as "Lord, It Hurts," a song included in this book.

"I felt very loved then by my heavenly Father," Carol said. "Even though I didn't know where my earthly father was, I knew my heavenly Father was with me."

During the 1980s, seventeen of Carol's songs were sung by a young artist on *In the Morning: Songs of Inner Healing.* That cassette recording is no longer available, but most of those songs appear as poems in this book.

Carol also created letters she called "Envelope Hugs," often including handwritten copies of her poems and songs. She sometimes wrote to people she did not know and held workshops to encourage others to send inspirational and often-decorative Envelope Hugs.

Seeing her hand copying one of her poems, I said, "Let me type that and make copies for you."

"No, I want to write it," Carol said. "Sending something handwritten is more personal."

I hope her poems and passionate writing about Envelope Hugs inspire you. After reading, you perhaps may agree with Barbra Eschmann, Carol's friend, who wrote, "Carol, you wear your heart on your sleeve—and that's good since you have a strong instinct about matters of the heart."

—Larry Steve Crain

*Carol in her twenties, holding the watercolor of her dog, Heidi, that
her husband, Steve, painted for her when they were in college.*

Stumbling Block or
Stepping-Stone

May the hurts and disappointments of my life
Be a stumbling block or a stepping-stone?
Will I allow them to cause bitterness and strife,
Or will I let them strengthen me as I walk on?

It's up to me, what I let God do in my life.
The choice is mine—
To win or lose,
To be stable or confused.
The trials I've had in days gone by
Can make me quit or determined to try.
Lord, with your help,
I'll let them be a stepping-stone.

Don't Let Your Yesterdays Ruin Today

Don't let your yesterdays ruin today.
Don't let today
Put a cloud on tomorrow.
Don't let all your memories
Of the past and its mistakes
Continue to cause you
Pain and sorrow.

For what is behind you
Is part of the days gone by.
What good can it do you now
To continue to cry?
Don't let your yesterdays ruin today.
Don't let today
Put a cloud on tomorrow.

Don't let who you used to be
Keep you from who you are.
Don't let all your failings
Keep you from winning.
Don't let where you used to walk
Keep you from finding out
Jesus can give you
A brand-new beginning.

For what is behind you
Is part of the days gone by.
What good can it do you now
To continue to cry?
Don't let your yesterdays ruin today.
Don't let today
Put a cloud on tomorrow.

Clouds

God, take these clouds from my mind today.
They keep out your Son in a cruel, chilling way.
I need your warmth to release my mind
From these wretched thoughts that are so unkind.

I need to think of today and you
For my blessings are many; my disappointments are few.
So take these clouds from my mind, I pray.
Praise God, I can feel the clouds floating away.

And now I see that those memories
That chilled my poor soul
Don't have control.
For when I asked to be freed and healed,
You let your Son be my strength and shield.

He shields my heart from the hurting thoughts,
And I'll praise him for the good things he's wrought.
Just look how he has protected me
During all my past days in his loving ways.

Day before Yesterday

Day before yesterday
Life didn't go my way.
Now I carry those memories
Around on my shoulders.

Forgetting is so hard to do.
Lord, I need you to
Help me get through
And show me your perfect way
To deal with
Day before yesterday.

Often I'm so weighed down.
Life's not a smile—
It's a frown.
My day before yesterdays
Are with me today.

Of the past I must learn to let go.
Lord, use me your love to show,
And give me a peace that will stay
When I'm reminded of
Day before yesterday.

Help Me Be Quiet Inside

Help me be quiet inside.
Lord, help me calm down.

Although I am saved from my sin,
Too often I'm bound.

Bound by the cares of this life
And the pressures within.

Help me trust you, precious Lord,
My victory to win.

Help me be quiet inside.
Lord, give me release.

From the chains of a worrying mind,
Give me thy peace.

For I know I'll fail on my own,
Apart from your touch.

Help me be quiet inside.
Lord, I need you so much.

Carol as a baby with her mother in California.

Is There Anyone?

Is there anyone alive
Without a permanent scar
Affecting who they truly are?

Is there anyone alive
Who's never known pain
Tearing their heart,
Leaving a stain?

Is there anyone alive
Who got away scot-free
From life's hurts?
Not you or me.

But we know the Savior,
Who can heal all our loss
Because he gave all
On his Father's cross.

Is there anyone alive
Whom he won't receive?
Not one; he'll save all
Who will trust and believe.

My Feelings

When I read my feelings
Written down,
They're harder to deny.
And I
Feel the need
To write my thoughts
As they flow,
So I will more
Deeply, fully know
My feelings.

Song of My Feelings

Let this song of my feelings
Look inside and bring you healing
Of a memory or two
That keeps bringing hurt to you.

Let these words from my heart
Teach you how you can start
To put the past all behind
With God's help.

For everyone has a song
They can write.
Everyone has come through
Blackest nights.

Let Jesus help you write your song;
The words he'll give you will belong.
He'll make them rhyme
And give them meaning
When he helps you write your song.

He'll make the answers
Fit life's questions
You've been asking for so long.
He'll heal your memories
And give you peace
With his song.

For everyone has a song
They can write.
Everyone has come through
Blackest nights.

Let Jesus help you write your song;
The words he'll give you will belong.
He'll make them rhyme
And give them meaning
When he helps you write your song.

Me

There's so much
I can't begin to tell you
About all the pain
I'm going through.
How I'm hurting
So deep within.
Will I be the same again?
Will I ever be the same
Person again?

It seems
I've been losing
My identity,
And yet I'm just discovering
The real me.
As I keep on searching
And looking for the whys,
Lord, the blinders
Are being taken from my eyes.

The light's often painful,
Yet, Lord, somehow I know
The picture revealed will help me to grow
Into the person
That I long to be …
The person
Who lives
Deep within me.

Help Me to Forgive Myself

Lord, you know the hurt I feel
For being who I was.

Help me to forgive myself,
Relieve my pain because …

I know I can never be
Who I'm meant to be in thee
Until I can forgive myself
For being who I was.

Heal my memories from my past.
Help me daily see
That when you died on Calvary,
You died to set me free.
'Cause I know I can never do
All the things you've asked me to
Until I can forgive myself
For being who I was.

You Never Left Me

When I look back at my life,
I see many things.
There were so many bad days
When I couldn't sing.
But now I can realize
And far better see
That you were right with me.
Lord, you never left me.

You never left me
When the hurts came along.
You never left me.
Now you give me new songs
To tell of your working
And healing in me.
Oh, Jesus, I'm thankful
You never left me.

Jesus Christ the same yesterday, and today, and forever.
—Hebrews 13:8 (KJV)

Take Away

Lord,
Take away my disappointment.
Take away my hurt, I pray.

Take away all the scars;
Only you know what they are.
Lord, I'm asking now
In faith, believing
For you to have your way.

Lord,
Take away the things that hinder me;
Please remove them from my heart.

Let my mind be healed, and make me whole.
And help me make a brand-new start.

Take away all the scars.
Only you know what they are.
Lord, I'm asking now
In faith, believing
For you to have your way.

Lord, I'm asking now
In faith, believing
For you to have your way.

Velvet Cords

Lord, you wrapped me
In your velvet cords
To support me
When the ropes of life
Seemed ready to hang me.
Your cords never left rope burns
Caused by leaving me
Twisting in the wind.
Your velvet cords
Held me up and
Strengthened me
As I learned to trust
Your love and grace.
Your velvet cords,
Though strong,
Were gentle around my life.

Lord, Sometimes

Lord, sometimes I'm cast down,
Turned inside out and around.

Unable to quite see
The way you've planned for me.

Unable, Lord, to know
Which way my life will go.

Then I pause and take a rest,
Knowing you will do what's best.

And once more I renew
All my faith and trust in you.

Lord, sometimes I'm unglued,
Often wondering what to do.

Sometimes all my peace
Vanishes as cares increase.

Sometimes I lose sight
Of your strength
And wondrous might.

When I do, Lord,
Speak to me.

Gently nudge my
Thoughts toward thee.

Give Me a Faith That Is Mine, Mine Alone

Lord, give me a faith
That is mine, mine alone.
Give me a faith to embrace
As my own,
Free from the reminders
Of past hurts and abuses,
Free from the memories
Of false piety and misuses.

Lord, set me free
To love and embrace thee;
Yet separate my heart
From those who have hurt me.

Oh, I want so much
To put distance between
All the distorted behavior I've seen
Displayed by those who said
They knew you.
I cry when I think of
What they put me through.

Lord, give me a faith
That is mine, mine alone.
Give me a faith to embrace
As my own.
Oh, Lord, please heal
My hurts from the past.

How I thank you
For giving me
Your peace that lasts.

Lord, You See Us

Lord, you see us
When we're wounded.
You see us when
We're hurting.
You see us in our pain,
When we cry inside.
Though we often look to others
As if we're doing okay,
And we try hard not to show
What we feel each day,
Lord, when all is
Said and done,
You,
You are the only one
Who sees beyond
The surface
Into who we really are.
Lord, you see beyond
The surface
Into who we really are.

Yesterday Is Gone

Lord, yesterday is gone
Yet not in the past.

Sometimes sad memories
Seem to last and last.

They suddenly show up;
They just seem to reappear.

And though they taunt us endlessly,
One thing is very clear.

You give peace in the midst of memories,
Peace that this world cannot give.

There's a reason we were permitted
To walk through those hailstorms of pain.

Lord, you've not let us suffer for nothing;
You've promised again and again.

And somehow when we share the lessons
You've taught us as we've looked to you,

The pain in our hearts heals more fully,
And we feel your love that renews.

Carol as a child in Pennsylvania.

Lord, It Hurts

Lord, it hurts; you know it hurts me
When I think of days gone by.
When I look at my life's pieces,
Oh, it often makes me cry.

I am asking you to heal me …
Heal the memories that hurt me so.
How I need your gentle soothing
You alone can really know.

Thank you for your reassurance
And your gift of love to me.
Without you my hurts are senseless,
And their meanings I can't see.

Lord, I praise you for the comfort
You are bringing to my soul.
As I open my heart to you,
By your touch I'll be made whole.

I Wish I Could Go Away

Lord, this shelter I have carefully built
To hide from all life's storms
Is too full of cracks and gaping holes.
It doesn't keep me warm.

I have spent so many hours
Searching for a peace that stays.
Lord, I have wished so often
That I could go away.

Go away from life's pressures and its people;
I'm not running from my feelings.
Lord, I need your light revealing
To shine upon me, give me healing,
Lord, I pray.

Give my tired soul release.
Fill me with your joy and peace.
Heal my memories with your love
More each day.

Lord, you know the meaning of my feelings.
You know the hurts I have
That need your healing.
You know my comings and my goings.
Lord, it's true,
And I'm leaning, yes, I'm leaning upon you.

Leaning on you,
Leaning on you,
Trusting your Word to see me through.

You know my comings and my goings.
Lord, it's true, and I'm leaning, yes,
I'm leaning upon you.

Saying Isn't All

Saying it's settled—the hurt is all gone—
Doesn't always mean the victory's been won.

Saying, "I'm fine … all is okay,"
Doesn't send deep-rooted memories away.

Saying is one thing—
Feeling another.

Admitting the hurting
Is the way to recover.

Recover from hurts that
Have set life aback.

Recover from the pain of
Satan's attack.

For only as we let God's love heal our pain
Can we ever be whole and live life once again.

Grey Days

Lord, I've had too many grey days—
Times of not being completely in darkness
Yet not enjoying the warmth of your light either.
Not in the ditch,
Yet not on the mountain.
Not in torment,
Yet not in peace.
Not in hatred,
Yet not in love either.
I walk an in-between road
Too many days, Lord.
Help me determine
To seek your power more
To enable me to
Cross over to the
Sunny side of the street!

Somewhere in the Middle

Somewhere in the middle
Of my mind's dark night,
I realized I didn't have to
Stay there.

Somewhere in the middle
Of my breaking heart,
Lord, I realized I could
Take your hand.

Take your hand
And walk with you
On life's pathway.
Take your hand
And walk with you
Down life's road.

For as I daily
Walk with you,
I know your love
Will see me through.
Lord, I know you'll never
Let me go.

Somewhere in the middle
Of my trials and cares,
I realized I didn't have to
To stay there.

Somewhere in the middle
Of my wounded soul,
Lord, I realized
I could take your hand.

Take your hand
And walk with you
Down life's pathway.
Take your hand
And let you guide me
Down life's road.

For as I daily walk with you,
I know your love will
See me through.
Lord, I know you'll never
Let me go.

Somewhere in the middle
Of my mind's dark night,
Lord, I realized you'll
Never let me go.

Looking Back

Lord, sometimes when I look back,
I see a winding road.

And I feel the weight of memories
That cause my heavy load.

I see the rocks I've stumbled on
As I've walked the road of faith.

Well, I look back too often, Lord,
When I should look to your face.

'Cause looking back
Only causes hurt and pain.
Looking back
Can't help me rise again.

Lord, help me look to you
For your Word, alone, so true,
Can help me spend every day
Not looking back.

I won't look back—no looking back.
There's no looking back for me.

I'll look ahead and
Walk with you, Lord,
Knowing I'm secure in thee
For looking back to the past
Doesn't give me peace that lasts.
I won't look back;
I'll look ahead
And walk with you.

Every Now and Then

Every now and then
The pain starts coming back
When I relive a memory
From the past.

Every now and then
I feel under attack,
And I wonder how long
This hurt's going to last.

Lord, help me give them all to you.
When they flood my mind,
Please give me peace anew.
May I learn how I can grow
When past memories hurt me so,
Not just every now and then,
But all the time.

Every now and then
I feel weighed down by life,
And problems seem to
Take away my peace.

Every now and then
I am caught up in such strife,
And I find it hard
My burdens to release.

Lord, help me give my cares to you.
When trials come, please
Give me peace anew.
May I learn how I can grow
When life's troubles toss me so,
Not just every now and then,
But all the time.

Every now and then
I lose sight of who I am
And think about the past
And what has been.

Every now and then
I forget what I have now,
And I think about the loss
My life has seen.

Lord, help me give the
Past to you
When what might have beens
Crowd into present days.
Lord, I learn more and more
Not to question "Why?" "What for?"
Not just every now and then
But all the time.

I'll Let Today Be a Brand-New Day

Lord, I'll let today be a
Brand-new day.
With your help, I'll put the past away.
I'll receive all you have
For me as I walk your way,
And I'll let today
Be a brand-new day.

Today will never come
This way again.
Today is your gift, Lord.
I know not when
I'll not have another
Day upon this earth.
So I'll live this day
For all it's worth,
And I'll let today
Be a brand-new day!

Carol at age five and a half, in 1953.

If I Could Know the Reasons

Lord, if I could know the reasons for my hurting,
I might not find my life so disconcerting.
If I could know the wherefores, then I would try
Not to spend so much time asking why.
But then again, suppose I know the causes of my pain.
I'd still find it necessary to forgive and start again.

I Can Sing in the Night

I have a Savior who knows everything.
He gives me life's answers when no one else can.
I have a Savior who knows me so well.
His love dries my tears and gives me songs to sing.

I can sing in the night when I cannot see the light.
I can sing when my troubles surround me
For Jesus is my light; he's my ever-present help.
His power strengthens me as he wraps his arms around me.

I can sing, I can sing, I can sing in the night.
I can sing, I can sing for Jesus is my light.
I can sing in the night when I cannot see the light.
I can sing for Jesus is my light.

I'd Never Choose to Cry

Lord, I know I would never choose to cry.
I know I would never order pain.
I'd always choose the sunshine—
I'd never choose the rain.
If I could have my way,
I'd never choose to cry.

Lord, I know I'd never choose
A mountain to climb.
I know I would never choose
The hard path.
But after I have realized
That the times when I've grown strongest
Were not in fields of flowers
But as I've climbed trial's mountain,
Lord, my Lord, I will trust you
To lead me where you choose.

Lord, my Lord,
I will trust you every day
For I know if I do,
I will always win, not lose.
So Lord, I will trust you.
I will trust you every day.
For I know if I do,
I will always win, not lose.
So Lord, I will trust you.
I will trust you every day.

Hurting Yesterdays

I'm thinking, Lord, of hurting yesterdays.
Oh, how their memories flood my mind.
I'm asking you to take the pain away
For you alone can help me find

My life's purpose and direction.
Peace and joy, come what may.
Lord, I need your loving touch upon my heart
To heal the pain of yesterday, yesterday.

I know I cannot make it on my own;
The wounds are deeper than I know.
The memories of my hurting yesterdays
Hammer at me b-l-o-w by b-l-o-w.

Lord, I must take your shield upon me.
If I would conquer the foe,
I must fill my mind with your Word.
When I do, the enemy will go; this I know!

I know—and I'll be healed
From the pain of yesterday.

Right Now

Lord, right now
There's so much
I don't understand.
But someday I will.

Right now there's so much
Confusion.
But someday the
Clouds will clear.

Right now there's so much
I can't explain.
But someday, Jesus,
I know you will.

Lord, help me right now
To trust you for
Understanding ...
Someday.

I Will Not Be Shaken

I will not be shaken.
I will not fall back.
Lord, I will count my blessings,
Not look at what I lack.
Though sometimes I don't know why
Things happen as they do,
I will hold your hand, Lord,
And give my cares to you.

I will not be shaken.
I will not look down.
Lord, I will sense your presence
In me and all around.
I am your child, and I know
Your promises are true.
I will hold your hand, Lord,
And give my cares to you.
I will not be shaken.
I'll give my cares to you.

Hand Them All Over to God

Hand them all over to God—
Your guilts and your memories
That keep on reminding you
Of days that are past.

Hand them all over to God;
Let his power relieve you.
He'll give you his peace, joy, and love—
The kind that will last!

Hand them all over to God—
Your worries and burdens.
Hand them all over to God.
His love is so kind.

For as you relinquish your cares,
You'll know him more fully.
Hand them all over to God;
Let him ease your mind.

Today, Lord, and Tomorrow

Lord, separate me
From the sorrows of my past.
Give me peace
And joy that ever lasts.
Help me know your love more
Every day.

Separate me
From my past, I pray.
For sometimes
I feel heaviness within.
Sometimes I'm unable
To begin
To do the work
You've called me forth to do.
Help me, Lord,
To give my past to you.

Separate me
From my hurt and pain.
Give me hope
To start anew, again.
For only as I let you
Heal my sorrow
Will I be able
To live for you
Today, Lord,
And tomorrow.

Through Him I Can Face
Each New Day

There are dreams
I have lost
That I may never find.
There are hopes that have shattered
When life has been unkind.
There are times when I wonder
How I can go on.
But then God reminds me
That is why he sent his Son.

In my problems and cares,
He is with me—always there.
In my disappointments, too,
Jesus comes to see me through.
When he died for my sin,
He gave me power to win,
And through him I can face
Each new day.

There are plans I have made
That just have not worked out.
There are dark days sometimes
That I walk through in doubt.
There are hurts that I feel
Deep down, from my past.
But Jesus reminds me
Only his peace can last.
In my problems and cares
He is with me—always there.
In my disappointments, too,
Jesus comes to see me through.
When he died for my sin,
He gave me power to win,
And through him, I can face
Each new day.

My Times Are in Your Hands

Sometimes I have worried
And my heart's been filled with fear,
Wondering what was going to happen
And how soon my death was near.

When the doctor gave his verdict
And said, "Here's what my tests show,"
I felt the Lord's peace with me
And said, "This one thing I know."

My times are in your hands,
Lord, my times are in your hands.
I know my times are in your hands.
I don't know I'll never suffer.
I don't know I'll not have pain,
But my times are your hands,
And I can sing it once again.

Lord, when I walk through the fire
And when I forge through the flood,
I will be led safely through
For there's power in your blood.

And no matter what takes place
Within my body, Lord, it's true,
Your Spirit dwells within me,
And peace fills me through and through.

Lord, my times are in your hands.
My times are in your hands.
I know my times are in your hands.
I don't know I'll never suffer.
I don't know I'll not have pain,
But my times are forever,
Yes, they are forever.
My times are forever in your hands.

Jesus, You Are Life

Jesus, you are life.
It is only through you we can live.

Jesus, you are love.
It is only though you we can love.

Jesus, you are hope.
It is only through you we can hope.

Jesus, you are life,
You are love,
You are hope.

Jesus, you are life, you are love, you are hope!

He Gives a Song

He gives a song in days of trial;
He gives a song during dark despair.

When troubles come to stay awhile,
We can sing because we know our Lord is there.

Our Lord is there to give us strength
For our burdens he will share.
We can know his arms uphold us
As we walk life's way.

Our Lord is there to give us peace;
He still hears and answers prayer.
We can sing his song of
Victory and power.

For he gives a song in days of trial;
He gives a song during dark despair.

When troubles come to stay awhile,
We can sing because we know our Lord is there.

Yes, we can sing his song of victory and power.

In the *Mean*time

Lord, I'm trusting you to
Remove the darkness that has
Settled over my life.

But in the *mean*time,
While the shadows deepen,
I will trust you to walk
Through it with me.

Lord, I'm trusting you to
Heal the disease in my
Body that poses a threat
To my life.

But in the *mean*time,
While tests and surgery become
A part of my days,
I will trust you to give me
Peace as I walk through them.

Lord, I'm trusting you
To let me know the
Freedom from these tightening
Chains of fear and anxiety.

But in the *mean*time,
When I feel afraid,
I will seek your rest,
Your peace,
Your help.

For sometimes we are
Not transported from
The tragedies.
For however long
We are permitted to
Walk through them—
Knowing every moment,
Every hour, every day—
In the *mean*time,
We are never alone.

Today

Today,
Looking back at yesterdays,
I see past pages written
As I lived those days, made mistakes,
Enjoyed the joys,
And learned from the falling down
And getting up times.

Today,
Looking back at yesterdays,
I see I often lose too much of *now*
Thinking of *then.*
I diminish the present
By magnifying the past.

Lord, help me let go of what has happened,
So I can embrace and nurture
What *is*
This moment!

Peace in the Midst of the Pain

Lord, sometimes life's hurts
Come against me
And knock me sideways and backwards
Once again.

Then you remind me you're with me,
And you'll help me.
You'll help me have peace
In the midst of my pain.

I don't have to wait
Till the problems have vanished
And can wound me no more.

I can move forward
In the midst of …
Move forward
In the midst of …
I can move forward
In the midst of
My pain.

Lord, When

Lord, when I receive your peace
I am severed and released
From the pain that tightly binds me
And keeps me down and out.

I'm reminded of your love, Lord,
How you're with me
By the power of your Word.
If I listen to your voice,
I'll lose my doubt—

The doubt that floods my thinking
And makes me fear I am sinking.
That doubt is banished
As I heed your voice.

You remind me of your power,
And you let me know each hour
That I can know your peace.
But it's my choice.

I can dwell upon the pain
Or let your peace fall like rain
Upon my thirsty spirit,
Oh, so dry.

I can think on things on earth
Or choose to dwell on
What I'm worth
And can reach my praises
Upward to the sky.

I Will Rest in You, O Lord

I will rest in you, O Lord,
No matter what my day brings forth
For I know how much I'm worth—
Far more than the sparrow.

You see it when it falls to the ground.
I know you see how my trials abound.
In you alone can peace be found.
So Lord, I will trust you.

Though darkness hovers over me,
Lord, I know you are within me.
When I walk paths too dark to see,
Lord, I know you are there.

So I will trust in you, O Lord,
No matter what my day brings forth.
I know how much I'm worth—
Far more than the sparrow.

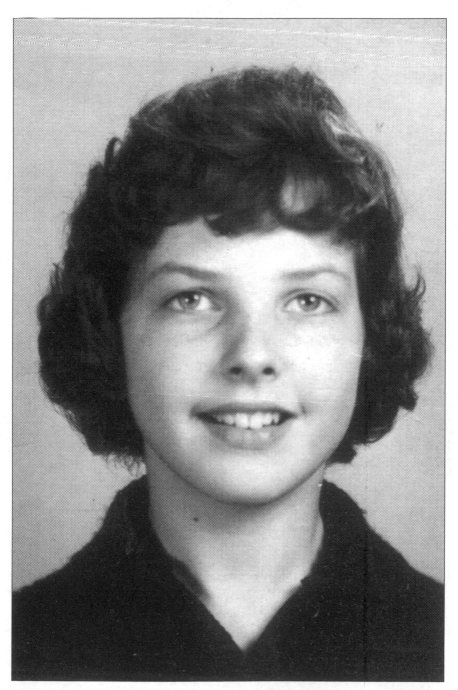

Thirteen-year-old Carol in Pennsylvania.

Old Memories

Old memories often overlap
Into my thoughts of now.
Memories of the hurts gone by—
Oh, Lord, please show me how
To let you further heal my pain
And take the sting from sorrow.
For if the old o'er takes the new,
I can't have peace tomorrow.

If I'm cast down by what life *was,*
Not dwelling on what *is,*
I cannot do your will for me;
Lord, I cannot your love give.
For time alone won't heal.
That timeworn phrase won't do.
But Lord, I know your power can heal
As I give my hurts to you.

Return with Me, Jesus

Return with me, Jesus,
To days that are past.

Walk down roads where I've been.
Give me peace that will last.

Return with me, Jesus,
A little each day.

For my present is tied
To the hurts I have known.
My feelings keep falling
Through the tears that need sewn.

Go back with me, Jesus,
So I might go forth
To learn who I am
And how much I'm worth.
Go back with me, Jesus.
Heal my memories, I pray.
Return with me, Jesus, a little each day.

Lord, You Saw Me

Lord, you saw my face
Before time began.

You knew that I would
Take part in your plan.

Lord, you saw my life
Before I was born.

You knew that I
Would trod your path well-worn.

The path so many have walked before
Has made all the difference
And means more and more.

As I realize anew
Who I am, Lord, in you,
I can face my life's trails and tests.

Lord, you saw my need
Before heartache came.

You knew how to heal
Memories that made me lame.

Lord, you shaped my future
And freed me from the past

By giving me your love
And a peace that would last.

A peace that this world can never erase,
That comes from accepting
Your wondrous saving grace.

As I realize anew
Who I am, Lord, in you,
I can face my life's trials and tests.

Someday

Lord,
Right now
There's so much
I don't understand,
But someday I will.
Right now there's
So much confusion,
But someday
The clouds will clear.
Right now there's so much
I can't explain,
But someday, Jesus,
I know you will.
Lord, help me, right now,
To trust you for understanding—
Someday.

More Often

I still feel the sting
Of life's pain.
I still wish for sunshine,
Not rain.
I still look at loss,
Not gain.
Lord, I still too often complain—
Way too often.
Help me think
On your blessings each day.
Help me focus
On your perfect way
More often.

Sometimes I Feel

Lord, sometimes I feel like the sun won't shine again.
Sometimes I feel so alone, apart from friends.
Sometimes I feel like the darkness will not end.
But then you speak to me and show me your love.

You speak to me in a smile from a baby.
You speak to me in the fragrance of a flower.
You speak to me when my life is filled with maybes …
In my darkest, most needy hour.

Lord, when I feel like the sun won't shine again,
Lord, when I feel so alone, apart from friends,
Lord, when I feel like the darkness will not end,
You speak to me and show me your love.

You speak to me and show me your love.
Lord, you speak to me and show me your love.

Many Are Hurting

So many are hurting,
Yet their wounds they disguise.
But if you look more closely,
You'll see pain in their eyes.

Take time to listen.
Be gentle; don't shove!
Help them reach out for
God's mercy and love.

I Could Not Live a Day
without Your Help

In a world that's filled with problems,
Turmoil, and distress,
Lord, I often call upon you,
Seeking peace and rest.

And every day I am reminded
That you know what's best.
I could not live a day
Without your help.

Lord, I could not live a day
Without your help.
I could not live a day
Without your help.
Every day I and reminded
For me, you know what's best.
Lord, I could not live a day
Without your help.

Lord, I could not live a day
Without your help.
I could not live a day
Without your help.
You are the very best friend
I have ever, ever known.
Lord, I could not live a day
Without your help.

There'll Be Light in the Morning for You

There'll be light in the morning for you.
You can trust God to see you through.
Though Satan brings doubts, the Lord will lead you out,
And there'll be light in the morning for you.

Jesus loves you, and he holds your hand.
He'll not give you more than you can stand.
And someday you'll see why all this was meant to be.
Yes, there'll be light in the morning for you.

Sometimes you'll feel like you can't take the pain,
But Jesus gives far more sunshine than rain.
Yes, he cares for you, and his grace will see you through.
There'll be light in the morning for you.

There'll be light in the morning for you.
You can trust God to see you through.
Though Satan brings doubts, the Lord will lead you out,
And there'll be light in the morning for you.

Help Me Look to You, Lord

Looking straight into the rays of wrongs that
Cannot be made right

Often blurs my vision, Lord, and
Dulls and dims my sight.

Looking straight into the rays of
Hurts unjustifiable

Brings me face-to-face with thoughts
And feelings undeniable.

Lord, help me not to look into
The face of days gone by.

Help me look to you, my Lord,
For the answers to life's whys.

To Him I Must Go

When I am down
And troubles abound,
My Lord lets me know
To him I must go.

When with him I share
The burdens I bear.
I've comfort and peace
For I'm in his care.

To him I must go.
To him I must go;
For he alone knows
What I'm going through.

To him I must go.
To him I must go;
For I know my Lord
Knows just what to do.

When plans go awry
And I question, "Why?"
My Lord lets me know
To him I must go.

He makes no mistakes;
For the paths that I take
Are shaped by his hand,
Though I don't understand.

To him I must go,
To him I must go
For he alone knows
What I'm going through.

To him I must go,
To him I must go
For I know my Lord
Knows just what to do.

Let Them All Go

Let them all go.
Let your troubles and cares all go.
Lay them down at Jesus's feet.

Let them all go.
Let your burdens and worries go.
Lay them down at Jesus's feet.

Then your mind will be free
To think of him.
Let him lift your load off your shoulders.

You can be at peace with him
If you let them all go.
Let them all go.

Let them all go.
Let your doubts and fears all go.
Lay them down at Jesus's feet.

Let them all go.
Let your sorrows and griefs all go.
Let Jesus make you whole and complete.

Then your mind will be free
To think of him.
Let him lift your load off your shoulders.

You can be at peace with him
If you let them all go.
Let them all go.

We Shall Not Have These Heartaches Anymore

When one day we meet our Savior face-to-face,
All our earthly trails his presence will erase.
For just one look at him—so filled with his love—
Will turn our thoughts toward heaven
And things above.

And we shall not—no, we shall not—
Have these heartaches anymore.
We shall not cry tears
From a wounded heart that's torn.

So let us run life's daily race.
Let us picture our Lord's face
Always before us—leading us on—
To where we shall not
Have these heartaches anymore.

Let us press on; let us press on
'Til the victory we have won,
Knowing one day we'll
See the face of God's Son.

But in the meantime, we can know
He's with us where'er we go.
In the meantime, we can feel
His presence, oh, so real.

He walks with us in life's race,
And one day we'll see His face.
Yes, one day we'll see our Savior face-to-face.
One glad day we'll see our Savior
Face-to-face.

If I Knew That I

Lord, if I knew that I
Would never have to hurt again,
Would I readily accept a life
Free from further pain?

If I knew that I could spend my days
Doing just whate'er I please,
Would I readily accept a life
Of constant tranquil ease?

If I could have my way, Lord,
I know I would be weak.
I would choose constant sunshine;
No hardships would I seek.

Though you know this about me,
You allow me to endure
Times of hurt and trial
To make my faith more sure.

For Lord, you know
I would not grow
If I never walked in rain.
You know my faith would never rise
Above earth's level plain.

As You Walk

As you walk down life's pathway of trials,
Remember God's there by your side,
Helping you come through victoriously
As you are tossed, tempted, and tried.

For when you asked his Son to save you,
He promised that he'd carry you
Through all the tests and dilemmas
The god of this world puts you through.

So rejoice though your path may seem rocky.
Praise him though your way may be rough.
For because you're his child, he will show you
His grace is far more than enough.

So don't worry about your tomorrows,
And stay worn out from living each day.
Don't fret o'er the world that surrounds you.
Just trust God to show you his Way.

I'm Not Alone

There are times in my life
When I don't understand.
But I can know when I have trials
God is there to hold my hand.

As I walk through life's hurts
And at times question why,
I can know the Lord will dry
Every tear from my eyes.

Yes, I know I'm not alone.
The Lord is with me every day.
I know I'm not alone.
Because of Jesus I can say,
"No matter what takes place
In my life each day,
The Lord will guide me through
As I walk with him and obey."

Even when
I feel alone,
I remember he's there
To bear my every burden
And share my every care.

Yes, I know I'm not alone.
The Lord is with me every day.
I know I'm not alone.
The Lord is with me every day.

To Cindy

God holds tomorrow
Securely in His hands.
He'll never give us more
Than we can stand.
When we are driven
To run ahead
Of this moment's open door,
God reminds us
We must live today
And enjoy
All it's put here for.

I Can't See Very Far Ahead

I can't see very far ahead
As I walk down life's road.
But I know Jesus holds my hand
And bears my heavy load.

I can't see very far ahead,
And sometimes I have doubts.
But then my Lord speaks peace to me
And always brings me out.

I can't see very far ahead,
But I know I must go
One step at a time with Christ,
The One who loves me so.

I can't see very far ahead,
But I know I can be
Sure of the One who leads me on
Throughout eternity!

Rest in Him

Whatever you're going through,
Today—in each minute—
You can be sure to know that
God's hand is in it.

For you are his child,
And you'll always know
That Jesus is with you
Wherever you go.

There's nothing too hard
For God's almighty hand.
He formed all the waters
And shaped the dry land.

Your life has a purpose.
As you seek his will,
You'll find peace and joy.
Rest in him and be still.

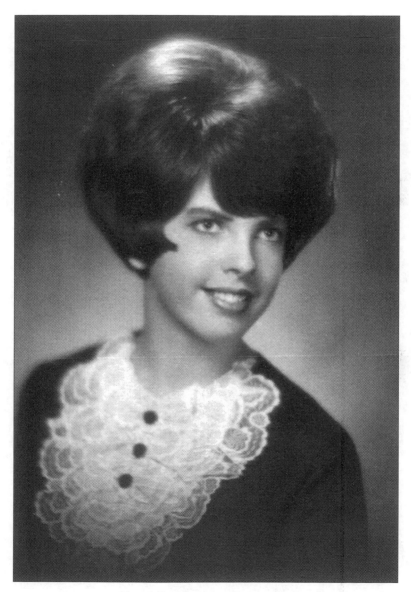

Carol during her college years.

More Comfort than All

I can receive comfort
From a friend's kind words.
I can receive comfort
From a song I've heard.
But this is one thing I know, Lord,
When on thee I call,
You give far more comfort,
More comfort than all.

You are my Father;
I am your child.
Your love is tender,
Gentle, and mild.

If I cling to you, Lord,
I will never fall.
For you give more comfort,
More comfort than all.

You ease my loneliness
And calm my doubts and fears
By letting me know
You are always near.

Yes, you give more comfort,
More comfort than all.
Help me, Lord, to trust you
And give you my all.
Help me, Lord, to trust you
And give you my all.

Take My Hand

Lord, take my hand
For I'm so afraid
Of what's ahead
In this world so full of sorrow.

Take my hand,
Lord, help me stand.
May I stay in your will forevermore.

Lord, walk with me.
Daily help me stand.
With you beside me,
I'll not worry o'er tomorrow.

Take my hand,
Lord, help me stand.
May I stay in your will forevermore.

Without Him

Oh, how utterly empty
My life would be
Without him, without him.

I would always feel tossed—
Like a ship on the sea—
Without him, without him.

Without him
As my Savior,
Who gives me security,
I would be only part of
The person
He'd planned me to be.

And I'd never have known
The true joy that I've found
If I had been
Without him, without him.

Tomorrow Doesn't Scare
Me Anymore

When I look around at this world,
Sometimes I worry and feel sad,
Wondering what will finally happen.
How will good days come from bad?

When I get a sinking feeling
Way down deep within my soul,
I remember I'm God's child;
He's in control.

So tomorrow doesn't scare me
Anymore, anymore.
For I know my Lord
Knows what's in store.

In his Word
He tells about my final destination,
So I don't worry,
No matter what my situation.

I'm reminded I must daily look to him
And take his hand.
As he walks with me,
I know my faith will always stand.

Tomorrow doesn't scare me
Anymore, anymore.
For I know my Lord
Knows what's in store.

My Affirmation of Faith

I have rejected the Christianity presented to me by
Certain ministers,
Certain writers,
Certain denominations.

But I have embraced the Christianity presented to me
by Jesus.

His love has remained real amidst the religious fog.
His peace has kept me consoled when no human words
could.

There are many things in life I am not certain of—as
well as people,
But I am sure that Jesus is who he says he is in the Bible.

I accepted him into my heart; he is with me … in me …
part of me.

No matter how many times I get thrown by life's hurts,
His understanding is never-ending.

Jesus is not a crutch; he is love, he is strength, he is a
friend and
Savior to all who will say, "I need you, Jesus. I'm not
self-sufficient.
I need your caring and guidance to help through life
and meet me in death."

Your Peace Is Mine, Lord

Lord, when I'm oh, so weary,
And I'm feeling down,
Help me sense your presence
In me and all around,
Letting me know I can
Be who I'm meant to be.
No matter what my pain is,
Through you I've victory.
Your strength is mine, Lord,
I know it's true.
You're always with me,
Showing me what to do.
Your peace is mine, Lord,
I trust in you.
Lord, your peace is mine,
Your peace is mine.
I trust in you, Lord,
Your peace is mine.

All True Comfort Comes from Him

Whatever I need, he has the supply.
Where I am, I'm watched by his eye.

Though I cannot see my Lord's loving face,
I know he is giving me his strengthening grace.

For all true comfort comes from him
When sorrow, pain, and heartache come my way.

All true comfort comes from him;
In darkness, Jesus helps me see the light of day.

When faced with life's problems, I know he is there.
During every trial, I know Jesus cares.

Though I cannot reach out and touch or take his hand,
I know he walks with me and ever helps me stand.

For all true comfort comes from him
When sorrows, pain, and heartache come my way.

All true comfort comes from him;
In darkness, Jesus helps me see the light of day.

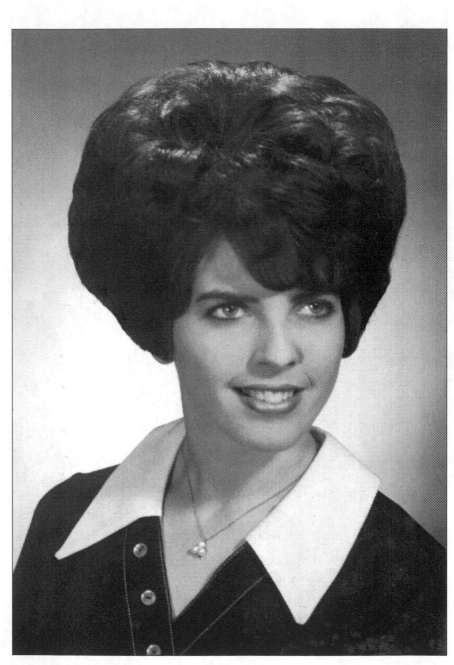

Carol during her years as a college student.

Just for Being There

Just for being there,
Father, I thank you.
Just for showing you care,
Father, I thank you.
I know I would be
So lost without thee,
So I'm kneeling in prayer
Just to say, "Thank you."

Just for loving me.

Just for setting me free.

It Won't Matter Much at All

Now I often think about the past
And all its pain.

Now I often wish for sunshine
While watching falling rain.

But someday,
When I see you, Lord,

And I hear your sweet voice call,
Then it won't matter;
It just won't matter much at all.

No, it won't matter at all.
My trials and hurts
Won't loom so tall.

When I see you, Lord,
And hold your hand,
Then you will help me understand,
And it won't matter at all.

My hurts won't
Matter at all.
My cares won't matter
Much at all.

My hurts won't matter.
My cares won't matter
Much at all.

When I Consider

When I consider the fact
That I'm one of millions,
God, it means so much
Knowing you care.

You see me each moment;
You know what I'm feeling.
There's never a second
That you are not there.

I am important to you;
This I know.
You gave your Son
Because you love me so!

Though I'm only one,
There's so much I can be.
I can show love to others
As you've shown your love to me.

For I am unique in your sight.
I'm not weak; I'm empowered by your might.
So many are feeling all alone;
They need you to guide them safely home.

Though I am not famous,
There's much I can do
To share your love with those
Who need you.

I Can Count on You

Lord, sometimes when I go through a trial
And its purpose I don't understand,
When the answer won't come,
And the victory's not been won,
I still know you are
Holding my hand.

Lord, I can count on you.
I can count on you.
I know you're there;
You will not turn away.

I can count on you.
Lord, I can count on you
To help me win
My life's battles each day.

I can trust in your Word
And your promise.
During my valley
You will be my light
For you've always proven true.
No matter what I've gone through,
Because you're with me,
I can face the darkest night.

Lord, I can count on you.
I can count on you.
I know you're there;
You will not turn away.

I can count on you.
Lord, I can count on you
To help me win
My life's battles each day.

Christ Brings Comfort

In all our affliction,
In all our pain,
Our Lord brings us comfort
Again and again.
His caring's not rationed
Or in short supply.
His love goes beyond
The height of the sky.
His Word speaks peace
To each troubled mind.
His grace gives hope
We could never find
In this world filled
With heartache and sin.

In all our affliction,
In all our affliction,
Christ brings comfort
Again and again.
In all our affliction,
In all our affliction,
Christ brings comfort
Again and again.

Carol in Aurora, Colorado, where her husband was stationed and where she taught a GED class for soldiers recovering from wounds.

In the Middle of My Valley

In the middle of my valley,
During the darkness of the night,
Lord, you always let me know
You are there to be my light!

You never told me
I wouldn't have sorrows,
But you have promised to
See me through.

When I am beset by
All of life's problems,
Lord, I must remember
To lean upon you.

In the middle of my trial,
During my worries and my cares,
Lord, you always let me know
My burdens you will share.

You never told me
I wouldn't have sorrows,
But you have promised
To see me through.

When I am beset
By all of life's problems,
Lord, I must remember
To lean upon you.

I must remember
To lean upon you.

Just When

Just when I'd had about all I could take,
Just when my heart felt as though it would break,
Just when my faith really began to shake,
God saw to it I was encouraged!

Just when my trials seem o'erwhelming to me,
Just when my hope seemed washed far out to sea,
Just when I thought the answer won't be,
God saw to it I was encouraged!

Just when—not before.
Just when I was unsure.
Just when I thought
I just couldn't endure,
God saw to it I was encouraged!

God is always on time, right down to the minute.
So remember—during each trial
That God's hand is in it.

He knows just when you need him to intervene.
We see what's at hand, but God sees the unseen.

No Problem Is Greater than You

When the sun goes down upon my life
And the sunrise seems so very far away,
I just call upon you, Lord, my source of light,
And then you turn my darkness into day.

When problems surround me and I'm burdened with care,
Lord, you're always with me; I know you are there.
If I walk with you, I know you'll see me through
For no problem in my life is greater than you.

Through Him I'm Free

The debt I owed to you, my heavenly Father,
Could not have been paid apart from Calvary.

How I praise you, oh, God, for sending Christ my Savior
To die that I might live eternally.

Through him I'm free from the weight
Of sin upon me.

Through him I'm cleansed from sin's stain
Upon my heart.

Oh, Father, when I try to put my feelings
Into words,

I'm so grateful
I don't know where to start!

Oh, Father, when I try to put my feelings
Into words,

I'm so grateful
I don't know where to start!

So Many People

So many people
Don't know the Savior.
They can't understand
Why life makes them cry.
But they always end up
Feeling empty inside.

Jesus can give them
True peace in their souls,
But they have to let him
Have complete control.
Satan will tell them
It just can't be done.
But millions have found out
Christ is truly God's Son.

So many people
Don't know the Savior.
That's why it's important
For all those who do
To share Jesus with them,
So they know he died
For their sins on Calvary,
And his Word is true.

To Be Absent

To be absent in the body
Is to be present with the Lord.
To be absent in the body
Is to be present with the Lord.

And you shall see your loved one again.
You shall see your loved one again.
If you know Jesus as your Savior,
You shall see your loved one again.

Now she's walking in God's heavenly light.
She needs no lamp as we do here.
And the angels sing Hallelujah
For her spirit is walking with the Lord.

And you shall see your loved one again.
You shall see your loved one again.
If you know Jesus as your Savior,
You shall see your loved one again.

For to be absent in the body
Is to be present with the Lord.
If you know Jesus as your Savior,
One day you'll be present with the Lord.

Feelings

I have a "know so" salvation.
I can feel it—it is real.
But if I could not feel it,
'Twould be the only way still.

My emotions may go up and down.
My feelings in … and … out.
Yet it matters not for he's my rock;
My Savior I'll not doubt!

I know that I'm not on a trip
Or a temporary high.
No matter what my feelings are,
The Lord to me is nigh.

Bending with the Wind

As I looked out my window, I saw a tree that was swaying so gently in the wind. Back and forth, back and forth, so willingly, and it brought forth the following response.

If a tree doesn't bend with the wind,
its branches will crack
and fall down.

When the wind blows in life, to and fro,
I must bend and learn
lessons profound.

For if I insist on my way and
refuse to let go and
let God,

the parts of my life God can use
will break off and get buried
in sod.

And there, in the sod of this world,
my life will take root and soon
die.

All because when God showed me his will,
I resisted and
would not comply.

God, help me bend with your leading.
I know I can't
make it alone.

My life needs your steadying guidance
so that I won't end up
being windblown.

Lord, Direct My Paths

Lord, direct my paths
Through the darkness
As I walk ways
Unknown to me.

Direct my path
Through the darkness
For I would stumble
Without thee.

This world is full of byways
Where your light so
Needs to shine.

How I pray you'll be
There with me
And clasp your hand
Around mine.

We Praise and Thank You

Lord, when the inner cores of our lives
Break and crumble,
When the earth beneath us
Starts to rumble,
When our feet slip and
We start to stumble,
Lord, your foundation is secure
Beneath it all
And will not let us fall.

When the voices of this world *rage*
And imprison us in a bondage cage,
You, Lord, will stay the same;
There is power in your name.
Lord, we are why you came.
You give us hope that makes us secure.
You keep our footsteps steady and sure.
For this, Lord, and so much more,
We praise and thank you.

How about You?

Some people are looking
At life's miseries today.
They wonder and question,
"Where is God anyway?"

But me, I just look at
Each beautiful flower
For I know he's with me.
Yes, I feel his power.

How about you?
Well, how about you?
Do you see life's flowers?
Do you feel his power?

No matter where you are
Or what you're going through,
Remember God cares, and
He's always with you.

Some people walk through
Their days feeling sad.
They can't see God's goodness.
Their world looks all bad.

But me—I just look up.
I refuse to look down.
And then I see Jesus;
His love's all around.

How about you?
Well, how about you?
Are you looking down,
Or do you look up?

You know if you'll ask him
He'll take your burdens,
And if you'll just let him,
He'll fill your cup.

So why don't you let him
Fill your cup?

He Is There

Sometimes you may feel
That life is too hard
And no one knows your plight.

Sometimes you may feel
So tired and worn out
From staying in the fight.

But when you have these
Pulling thoughts
That seem to take command,
Remember—oh, remember—
God is there to understand.

He's there to understand.
He's there to hold your hand.
Remember when
You feel alone, he is with you.

He's there to understand.
He's there to hold your hand.
You're not on your own
For he is there with you.

Sometimes in crowds
You often feel alone,
And you don't feel at home
When you're at home.

Sometime as day
Draws to a close,
You realize you're in pain
No one knows.

But when you have
These lonely thoughts
That seem to take command,
Remember—oh, remember—
God is there to understand.

He's there to understand.
He's there to hold your hand.
Remember, when you feel alone,
He is with you.

He understands.
He holds your hand.
Remember, when you feel alone,
He is with you.

Take Me, Dear Lord

Take me and break me and make me, dear Lord,
Just what you want me to be.
Give me the strength to do what you say
And eyes with the vision to see
All the proud, arrogant ways that I have,
And the many vain things that I do.
Make me aware that I'm often concerned
More with myself than with you.

Take me and break me and make me, dear Lord,
Just what you want me to be.
Help me lean on you and trust in your Word
To lead and direct and guide me.
For only as I'm led by you, precious Lord,
Can all that I do count for thee.
So take me and break and make me, dear Lord,
All that you'd have me to be.

Carol, pictured in 1971.

Not Knowing

Not knowing, I'll follow
Wherever God leads.
Not knowing tomorrow,
But he knows my needs.
So much of my walk is
To places unknown.
But as I go forth,
I am never alone.

Not knowing, yet knowing
That I can trust
In the God of creation,
Who made a man
Out of dust.
Not knowing, I'll follow
Wherever he leads.
Not knowing tomorrow,
But he knows my needs.

Not knowing, yet knowing
In him I can rest
As he shapes my future;
For me he knows best.
My life may seem aimless
At times as I go,
But in faith I'll follow.
Not knowing, I'll go.

You're the Same;
You Don't Change

Lord, there was a time
When my view of you
Was clouded by hurts
In my mind.

And I couldn't see
Your kind, loving face.
No peace in my life
Could I find.

I felt that I had gone
So far from you,
That you no longer
Even knew my name.

But then your love came through.
And it touched me, and I knew
That you were still
The same.

Lord, you're the same.
You don't change.
You're the same.
You don't change.

Yesterday, today, forever …
Lord, your love changes never.
I'm so thankful
You are always the same.

I Am Blessed to Be Yours

Lord, when I start to get down
And discouraged,
I think of the trials
You've brought me through.
Then my faith is increased,
And my burden's released.
Once again, Lord, I know
You'll see me through.
For you have never let go of my hand.
Your strength has always held me up
And let me stand!
As I keep my eyes on you,
Lord, your love will see me through.
No more distress for I am blessed
To be yours!
Amen and Amen.

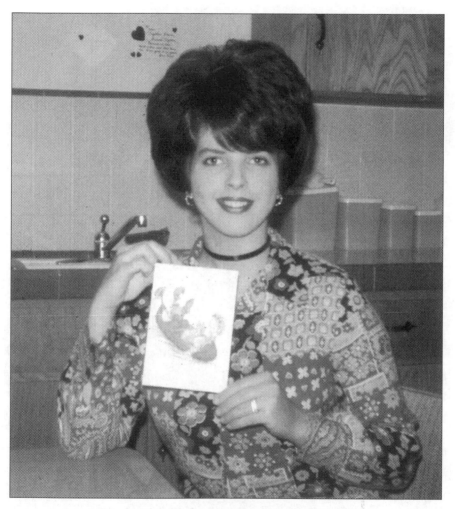

Carol with one of many greeting cards she sent.

Lord, My Faith's in Your Love without End

I don't know when my life will be over.
I don't know when my days here will end.
But I know, Lord, I will see you in heaven
For my faith's in your love without end.

Your love for us sent you to the cross.
You were willing to die for our sins
So that we might be able to spend the hereafter
With you, our Redeemer and Friend.

So I don't have to fear my last breath here.
I have peace in my heart every day.
For I know you are my Lord and Savior;
You're the truth, the life, and the way.

I don't know when my life will be over.
I don't know when my days here will end.
But I know, Lord, I will see you in heaven
For my faith's in your love without end.

In this world there is much that's uncertain.
Endless wars, loss of fortunes cause dismay.
Yet, Lord, I have peace and a sense of relief
When I think of what's coming my way.

When my life here is finally over,
My spirit will live on and on.
Though I'll no longer live on this earth, Lord,
I know I will never be gone.

I don't know when my life will be over.
I don't know when my days here will end.
But I know, Lord, I will see you in heaven
For my faith's in your love without end.
I know, Lord, I'll see you in heaven
For my faith's in your love without end.

Jesus, I Thank You for Your Love

Jesus, I thank you for loving me.
Jesus, I'm so glad you care.
Jesus, I thank you for saving me.
I know every moment
You're there.

Oh, Jesus!
You are my friend.
You've said you'll be with me
From beginning to end.

Someday when I cross
Death's river wide,
I know you will greet me
On the other side.

Then, Jesus, I will spend,
Jesus, I will spend,
Jesus, I will spend
All eternity with you.

Carol on Paris Mountain in Greenville, South Carolina.

Can You See?

Can you see yourself run free
From this tyranny of pain?
Can you hear yourself breathe easily
Though your problems still remain?
Can you feel your heart grow warmer
In the midst of winds so cold?
You can know all of this
If the Lord's hand you will hold.
For his love, his love will
Never let you go!

His power enables you to know—
To really know—
Just who you are
And how very much you're worth.
His plan gives purpose to
Your days and nights on earth.

Can you see him in your triumphs?
Can you see him during despair?
He is with you come what may.
The Lord is there; yes, he is there.
Look through his eyes and clearly see
The person he made you to be.

Can you see yourself
As the Lord made you to be?
Look through his eyes and clearly see
The person he made you to be.
Can you see yourself
As the Lord made you to be?

Lord in the Midst

Lord, in the midst of my problems,
In the midst of my pain,
I will let you use me
Again and again
To reach out to the hurting
Who are suffering great loss,
Reach out to the broken
To bring them to your cross.

Lord, I will share your love,
Mercy, and grace.
I will share your compassion;
That can help others face
Disappointments, tragedies, and pain.
I will reach out to others
Again and again.

For I know that in giving
I will receive
Strength to overcome.
Faith to believe,
Believe in your power;
That helps me overcome.

Believe in your strength;
That helps me not walk but run,
Run through the fire
And through heartbreak's flood
Knowing I am preserved
By the power of your blood.

Though I am unable to know
All life's whys,
Through your Spirit I'm able
To discern Satan's lies.
His lies say life's hopeless,
And my future is bleak.
Yet because of your truth, Lord,
With assurance I speak,
Saying I won't be shoved back
By life's fiery trials.
For I know, Lord, you're with me
All of the while.
Lord, I know you are with me
All of the while.

Moving On

Joys and losses, ups and downs—
We all have to learn to deal
With what's in our path,
Whether it's fair or not,
Whether we understand it or not.

So many times we see a problem
Ahead of us, in the road of life,
And we can only look at it as
An obstacle in our way,
Keeping us from moving on
In the direction we want to go.

But later—looking back—we can see
That the problem was a vehicle
That enabled us to move out of
The rut we'd been stuck in.
For only as we move on
In a stronger direction
Can we grow and realize
Our potential.
A situation that's not good for us,
Or a problem that keeps us in pain,
Can begin to feel like a familiar part of us,

And we're reluctant to try
The new pair of shoes
Because they have to be
Broken in.

If we seek to learn how
To get past our bitterness,
The resentment, the hurt,
Our feet outgrow the shoes
We're wearing, and they
Become uncomfortable.
But it seems easier and less painful
To stay where we are rather than move on.
It's hard to think about breaking in
New shoes, to walk on new paths.
But when we do leave the old behind
And move on in a new direction,
We feel so good; we are free to be
Ourselves more than ever!

When we let our memories pile up,
We get so cramped inside.
We have no more room to grow
And reach out and love.
Until we let the Lord reach into
Where we are and heal our hurts
From yesterday, we cannot reach
Out to others today and tomorrow.
Until we let the Lord reach into
Where we are and heal our hurts
From yesterday, we cannot move on.

Carol enjoys a birthday cake.

Today, before Tomorrow Comes

Lord,

Before tomorrow comes,
I want to say something about today.
Today is really a lot of yesterdays,
all stacked up like building blocks.

All the yesterdays aren't even mine, Lord.
Some belonged to my parents … and their parents …
And on and on it goes—way back,
yet so forward they come, those yesterdays.

They march relentlessly into the now,
like tattered, sacred soldiers out of battle.
Oh, some are decorated with the badges of happy memories,
but oftentimes, those seem to be overshadowed
by the bruised and broken soldiers.

It hardly seems fair, Lord, and I, I dwell too much
on those yesterdays. It's often evening before I really
take time to look at the "today" I've just bought
and paid for with hours of my life. Even while I am trying
to seize the beauty from today, the anxiety of tomorrow—
wondering, *What then?*—attempts to overtake me.

Lord, help me live each day fully. Keep me from missing
out on current blessings because I'm dwelling in yesterday's
stagnation. Help me not worry about tomorrow
for I know you have my future in your hand.
Yet sometimes I'm so driven to snatch it from you,
saying, "I want my way, now."

Teach me to wait, Savior. Guide me as I walk down life's road.
I don't want to take a detour into the past; nor do I want
to bulldoze my way ahead of you into the unknown future.
Help me walk step by step, Lord, day by day!

Thank You, God, for Ordinary Days

Thank you, God, for ordinary days
With ordinary things done in ordinary ways.
No fireworks
Or dazzle, just fireplaces
And buttered toast,
Hot dogs and marshmallows to roast.
The sun streaming through a windowpane,
Or drinking coffee while watching
Falling rain.
Hearing the hum of the washer and dryer,
Noticing my face in the mirror
As I admire
The person who looks back at me
And helps me recall all you, Lord,
Are and do.

Thank you, God, for ordinary days
With ordinary things
Done in ordinary ways.
No rhinestones or pearls,
Or feathers or fluff.
Just a day filled with blessings;
Though ordinary, they are enough.

My Salvation

(1 Peter 1:3–5)

My salvation is kept
By God each day
Beyond the reach
Of change and decay.
Nothing can snatch
This gift away
For I've Jesus within
My heart to stay.

Share

Lord, as we walk in a world
So full of valleys
And look around
At the sadness, sin, and loss,
May we be your hands extended
To the lonely,
And paint their way—every day—
To the cross.

For so many cannot see the cross.
It is shrouded by dark clouds
Of confusion.
Lord, let your light shine
Through each of us.
Please take away their unbelief
And disillusion.

Lord, you've reminded us
We cannot shun the dying.
From their hollow eyes
We cannot turn away.
Only as we share
Your wondrous message
Will they find you as
The truth, the life, the way.

Your Touch of Love

There are so many people
Who say they don't feel
Your love, precious Lord.
To them you're not real.

Help them know as I pray
And call their names today.
Help them know your
Touch of love.

For they're so lonely deep inside
Because your love they have denied.
Lord, help them to feel
Your presence so real.
Reach down and touch
Their hearts with your love.
Reach down and open their
Hearts with your touch of love.

Now Is All We Have

I know that
Now is all we have,
And today is all there is.

Tomorrow may never come,
So let's make each
Moment truly his.

God gives us life and breath
To lead the lost to him.
What are we doing with *now*?
So many are not in …

Not inside his fold,
Not cleansed of their sin,
Not forgiven of their sin.

Oh, tell them of God's love
And how he sent his Son
To die for every soul.
Yes, each and every one.

Tell them of his peace,
The joy that can be theirs.
Oh, let them know he cares—
For their souls he cares.

I know that
Now is all we have,
And today is all there is.

Redeem the time.
Each day redeem every minute
For your life is not your own.
It belongs to him.

Your life is not your own;
It belongs to him.

Lord, Shine Your Light

(Inspired by a visit to Dutchman Correctional Facility)

Lord, shine your light of guidance on me.
Shine your light of guidance on me.
As I walk life's pathway and sail stormy seas,
Oh, Lord, shine your light of guidance on me.

Lord, spread your love throughout my heart.
Spread your love throughout my heart.
As I your message to others impart,
Oh, Lord, spread your love throughout my heart.

Lord, keep your hand of protection on me.
Keep your hand of protection on me.
As I face temptation and dangers unseen,
Oh, Lord, keep your hand of protection on me.

Carol's grandparents' house in Pennsylvania as it appeared in the 1970s.

You've Never Gone Too Far Away

You've never gone too far away
For God to reach you with his love.
His caring and forgiveness
Engulf the seas, span skies above.
You've never been away too long
To once again travel home.
His arms are open;
He will claim you for his own.

For he's your Father, and he knows
About your hurts and wanderings.
He is your friend who understands,
And he alone can ever bring
Peace to your soul.
Give him control,
And always know
You've never gone too far away
For God to reach you with his love.

Sometimes it seems
The door is closed,
And you are too weak to get in.
But the roadblocks and the barriers
Are coming from your thoughts within.
And although the way seems steep
And the paths ahead too rough,
Keep trusting him;
His love won't fail you.
His strength's enough!

For he's your Father, and he knows
About your hurts and wanderings.
He is your friend who understands,
And he alone can ever bring
Peace to your soul.
Give him control,
And always know
You've never gone too far away
For God to reach you with his love.

House in Zollarsville, Pennsylvania

There's a little house
In Zollarsville
Where I've spent
Such happy days.
The memories
Stored in my mind
Flash back in many ways.
And even though I'm far away
From that little house back there,
Grandpap, you know
I love you lots
And that I'll always care.

Benjamin Newton Freeland Steele, Carol's grandfather, at his home in Zollarsville, Pennsylvania. He lived to be ninety-five years old.

Carol pictured with her grandfather, Benjamin Steele, in the 1970s.

The Third One of the Three

When the third one of the three of
Mother, Daddy, and me
Was taken away—
Cut off—
Out of the picture,
The two of us who were left—
Mother and me—
Were never really able to fill in
That gap,
That hole,
That space that was left
When Daddy left!

While somehow trying to make the empty space
Seem less vacant—less gaping—
We were only able to see the space between the two of us
Widen!

I always wished we could have moved toward each other
To make his vacancy seem less evident in our lives.
But somehow we were never able to.

She drew her hurt all to herself, like it was all hers,
And wouldn't let me share it; nor would she share mine.
I withdrew more and more into myself,
And the distance between us
Grew and grew.

The silence became deafening.
The small talk insisted upon became impossible to
accomplish.
The hard times we'd been through left us more strangers
Than sharers of each other's load.
Not being open, we became closed to each other.
When the third one of the three of
Mother, Daddy, and me
Was taken away,
The two who were left—Mother and me—became
Mother and me!

It's Hard to Celebrate Father's Day

It's hard to celebrate Father's Day
For a child whose father is away,
Unavailable and disconnected,
Showing no love
To a child he's rejected.

His support checks don't arrive.
There's no proof he's alive,
No proof he really cares.
For just what does he share?
Not his heart—or his wallet.
Such callousness.
What do you call it?

He lends no listening ear.
His abandonment makes it clear
That Father's Day is not
A day to celebrate,
Just a day when
His child feels second-rate.

A day to feel sad
About rejection and loss.
And don't forget the high
Emotional cost
Paid each lonely day
In innumerable ways
By a child who doesn't understand
Why there's no father's
Guiding hand,
While "Dad" gives no thought
For his
Child's pain
Caused by
Wondering and grieving
Again and again.

It's hard to celebrate Father's Day
For a child whose father is away.

Leaving

People leave
Wives,
Husbands,
Children,
Houses,
Jobs,
Churches,
Cars,
Schools,
Cities.

And yet, all too often—
In fact, most of the time—
They are shocked to discover
They cannot leave the one
Source of most of their
Problems:
They cannot leave themselves.

I Remember

I remember California.
It's the place where I was born.

I remember Pennsylvania
And the times I felt so torn.

I remember Carolina;
That's the place where I met you.

And I loved the very first time
You made my life feel brand new.

As I opened my heart to you,
I knew I'd never be the same.
We gave so much to each other,
Then you gave to me your name.

I remember Colorado,
Where our words all seemed to rhyme.
Then I remember writing letters
To a place so far from time.

I remember California,
Where once more I lived again,
For I'd completed a full circle
Wearing your gold wedding band.

Carol wrote "I Remember" in 1977 as a song for me. The song refers to Carol's California birthplace, her growing-up years in Pennsylvania, our college years in South Carolina, our marriage, my US Army service in Colorado and Vietnam, and my short army service in Salinas, California, at Fort Ord. We lived together while I was stationed at Fort Ord. From Salinas, where we lived, we drove to Oakland, California, where Carol had been born in 1947, while her father served in the army.

— L. Steve Crain

Carol and Steve Crain are pictured at Bethany Baptist Church, Travelers Rest, South Carolina, on their wedding day, August 20, 1970. The Rev. Ray Scruggs, pastor of that church, performed the ceremony.

Song for Steve

You have been just who I needed
During so many ins and outs.
You have been a patient listener
When I tired from problems' bouts.

When I felt worn out from trials,
You were there to help me win,
Win the battle o'er depression
And help me regroup again.

Words don't really paint the picture,
Showing how I feel for you.
Words can't ever share the depths of
All my special love so true.

I want to be just who you need
During this time when you feel so weak.
I want to let you know that my love
Is far too deep to merely speak.

My Baby Child

My baby child,
As you place your hand in mine,
How glad I am that I've
Put my hand in the Lord's.
For I know I can't lead you down
All life's many roads,
And so I've put your hand
In the Lord's.

As you get older,
And you take your hand from mine,
Thank God I know
You won't walk by yourself.
When you reach out to Jesus,
He'll be reaching back to you,
And you can walk hand-in-hand
With the Lord.

He'll never lead you astray
Or take you the wrong way.
You'll be safe, holding the hand
Of the Lord.

Carol and Steve Crain's first child, Janelle, playing in the front
yard of their home in Greenville, South Carolina, in 1975.

I Hope This Song Will Say

I hope this song will say
I love you in another way.
I'm so happy here with you;
It's where I belong!

For you were meant just for me.
I was meant just for you.
The happy times that we share
Make my dreams come true.

Because of who you are to me,
I'm far more able now to see
Who I am and who I want to be.
Your love's a gift from God to me.

And I hope this song will say
I love you in another way.
I'm so happy here with you;
It's where I belong!

Two Years Old and Singing

This poem was written on Saturday afternoon as I passed by the door and heard Janelle outside, playing happily in her dirt pile. (Carol, August 2, 1975)

> Just to hear you singing
> happily as you play.
>
> Just to watch you laughing
> in your ornery way.
>
> Just to know you're having fun
> and see that you're doing fine.
>
> Just to look into your eyes
> and see their glowing shine.
>
> Just to feel you kiss me
> with your little mouth so small.

Just to watch you growing:
My you're getting tall!

Just to hear you,
Just to see you,

Just to hold you—
What a pleasure!

O child of mine,
You are God's gift,
My priceless little treasure!

The Big Bed

A tiny little lady in such a great big bed.
As I stand here and look at you,
I feel a sense of dread.

For as I think your bed's so big,
As you're lying there,
What will the world be like to you

As you begin to dare
To venture out upon your own?
But Jesus will be there.

I know He watches over you
As you are fast asleep.
You haven't even turned two yet,

But He your soul will keep.
He'll be there when you start to school
And when you graduate.

He'll show you when to step right out
And teach you when to wait.
And He'll be there to guide you

When you meet that special "one."
His love for you is endless,
Warm as the morning sun.

So as I think of you, my child,
Asleep in your big bed,
My thoughts are far more peaceful now,
Since these few things I've said.

The Fall Tree

The fall tree is laughing
In the brightest colors
Ever seen,
Red and orange,
Brown and yellow.
Look at the expression
On that leafy fellow
As he proudly shows off
Nature's bright glory.
His outfit is priceless,
An ever-changing story.

His colorful splendor
Sways in the breeze.
None can match
His desire to please
All who see him
As they stand around,
Watching his costume
Falling down, down, down,
As he loses his colors
On the ground.

Although he feels a little sad,
He knows he's made
Many people glad.
So he looks ahead to next year,
Standing proud and tall,
Knowing once again
He'll be ablaze
With the beautiful colors of fall.

Just to Know

God led you to say something to me
In the hour of my deepest need.
Through your words, I felt God's
Sweet touch.
Oh, just to know—just to know that
He loves me that much!

Just to know that God cares
About all my needs.
Just to know that he shares
All my joys and my griefs.
Oh, just to know.
Just to know that
God loves me that much.

I received a friend's letter one day,
And its writer knew just what to say.
As I read it, I felt God's sweet touch.
Oh, just to know, just to know that
He loves me that much.

Many times my strength was renewed
When God reached me
Through someone like you.
Your kindness made me feel
God's sweet touch.
Oh, just to know, just to know
That God loves me that much.

Just to know that God cares
About all my needs.
Just to know that he shares
All my joys and my griefs.
Oh, just to know,
Just to know that
God loves me that much.

The Unknown Story

I saw a white-haired woman standing in
the Panera Bread parking lot today,
hugging a girl, who appeared to be in
her twenties, in a long embrace.
I wondered if the woman was a grandmother
who hadn't seen her granddaughter for a
long, long time.
As I drove around again, waiting
for a parking place to open up,
they were still holding each other.
The girl's face was facing me,
and she was crying.
I drove into a parking spot,
wondering. Everyone has a story.
I would have liked to have known
theirs.

Carol's beloved grandmother, Rose Ella White Steele.
She died while Carol was in college.

Carol spent lots of time with her maternal grandparents, Benjamin Newton Freeland Steele and Rose Ella White Steele, of Zollarsville, Washington County, Pennsylvania. Carol and her mother, Betty Day, lived in nearby Washington, the county seat.

About the following entry, Carol wrote in 2012,

> The below copy, taken from a postcard I found among my keepsakes, was written to me by my maternal grandmother, Rose Ella White Steele. The dog mentioned

was my Cubby. Cubby had to stay at Grandpa and Grandma Steele's house because I couldn't keep him in the apartment my mother and I occupied.

September 21, 1959 (date postmarked in Marianna, Pennsylvania, on a three-cent postcard)
From: Gramma Steele, Marianna Pa
To: Miss Carol Williamson, 103 E. Kathryn Ave., Washington Penna

Message:

Monday morning. Hi Honey. Well, I thought you like to know how the pup got along last nite. We put him in the shed not long after you left, just turned him loose and shut the door. I gave him some bread and milk and a flat bone from the roast we had. It had grease on it and you should have seen him gnawing on it. He didn't cry to amount to anything, just settled down and we didn't hear him all nite. I went out just now to feed him and he was still asleep in the corner on a sack. From now on I'm going to leave him in the room at nite. I don't think he will keep us awake and he will be warmer in here. I'll get him a collar when I go to town. I'll take good care of him. So don't worry.

Love,
Gram

My Grandma's Kitchen

I have many memories of my grandma's kitchen in Zollarsville, Pennsylvania.

My grandma, Rose Ella White Steele, baked little rolls she called "lightcakes." She also baked "salt-risin' bread" that had a strange smell. I didn't like that bread when I was a child, but after I married, I'd go to the local bakery where I lived in South Carolina and buy it at least once a year. I'd take it home and toast it and drink hot tea as I ate it. The smell of the bread in my house reminded me of my grandma, who died when I was nineteen.

Grandma also made cornstarch pudding in a pan on the stove. I remember standing and stirring the pudding with a wooden spoon. I stirred it until it thickened, so it wouldn't scorch and burn.

Grandma baked all kinds of pies in her kitchen. She made rhubarb pies from long rhubarb stalks that grew near the white fence in our neighbor Miss Martin's yard. Miss Martin let Gram have all the rhubarb she wanted. Gram would always give Miss Martin some of what she baked.

Gram also baked blackberry pies with berries she'd picked along the road and canned.

Most of all, I remember her pumpkin pies at Thanksgiving. They weren't spicy, which is why I liked them. I remember Gram taking her finger and "crimping" her piecrust so the extra dough around the edge would fall off.

I washed lots of dishes for Gram in her kitchen as I was growing up. I was glad to help her.

Grandma, Grandpap, and I sat around the Formica-topped kitchen table and ate our meals together. I have Gram's cream pitcher and my grandpap's sugar bowl, which sat on that table many years ago. They bring back good memories when I look at them now in my kitchen each day.

I Miss the Snow

Written by Carol on December 3, 1995, when she was a fifth-grade teacher and a Pennsylvanian living in North Carolina.

I miss the snow; it never comes
In great big flakes of fluff.
Once a winter snow dust may fall,
But that's just not enough.

I grew up playing in piles and drifts,
Making snowmen as tall as small trees.
How I'd love to do that again.
It would be such fun for me.

I'd put a big hat on his head
And a tall broom in his hand.
If I could build a snowman again,
Oh, that would be just grand.

Though Southern children wish and wish
For a snowstorm inches deep,
And hope before they go to bed
For a snowfall while they sleep.

They are disappointed
Year after year after year.
While Northern children play in piles and drifts,
It hardly seems quite fair.

A Childhood Wound Used to Help

Told by Carol to the late Muriel Larson, a writer and her friend.

My parents were divorced when I was two, and I never knew my father. Although I received Christ as my Savior at an early age, I could never see anything good that came out of my having to grow up in a broken home.

When teaching fifth grade in a rural school, I had an artistically gifted boy in my class. Mark loved to do bulletin boards and displays, and I developed a special feeling of warmth toward this creative child.

As the year progressed, however, I noticed he seemed increasingly troubled about something. It bothered me to see him gradually lose his enthusiasm for his creative work. One day Mark came to me after school and said, "I won't be in school tomorrow. I have to go to my grandmother's."

"Why?" I asked.

"My parents are going to court tomorrow to get a divorce," he answered. Then he started to cry.

I put my hand on his arm and said, "Well, Mark, I know how much this hurts you. My parents were divorced when I was not quite two years old, and it has hurt me a lot. I never even knew my father. But you have at least had yours with you for eleven years, and I'm sure he loves you and will keep in touch with you. Just because your parents are getting divorced doesn't mean you won't have a happy life. God has a purpose for your life, Mark. And even though this has happened to your parents, someday you can have a happy marriage just as I now have."

After Mark left, I sat there at my desk. I suddenly realized for the first time in my life I was thankful for what I had experienced because it enabled me to comfort Mark that day in the special way he needed.

I knew it wasn't God's perfect will for me to live in a broken home. But since it happened, He could use me to reach out to others—like Mark—who were being hurt as I had been.

That day I learned what the Word of God means when it says, "In everything give thanks" (1 Thessalonians 5:18).

Meant to Be

Carol wrote this to motivate her public school fourth-graders.

March is gone—where did it go?
April's here now—this I know.
Before I can turn around, I'll say,
"I can't believe the calendar says May."
June will be coming right behind.
Then July and August
Will be on my mind.
But for right now,
My mind can't rest.
I must push myself to do my best.
Each day is a gift for you and me
To use very wisely so we can see
Ourselves become
Who we're meant to be.

> Carol was a master teacher, and I can testify that she
> was an inspiration to her students and everyone who
> was lucky enough to have her touch their lives. (Connie
> Rogers, September 9, 2020).

Mrs. Rogers was a fellow teacher of Carol's when they taught at
Aberdeen Elementary School, Aberdeen, North Carolina. Carol
taught fourth- and fifth-grade classes there from August 1990 until
May 1998.

Carol and her first-grade teacher, Esther Clark.

From the Washington, Pennsylvania, *Observer-Reporter*, April 1998, (photo by Steve Crain):

Sweet Inspiration

Retired Washington schoolteacher Esther Clark, 87, received a visit from an admiring former student, one who was in her class of first-graders at Eighth Ward School in Washington almost 45 years ago.

"She was inspiring to me. I found stability and kindness in her classroom," says Carol Williamson Crain of Southern Pines, N.C. Mrs. Crain, who teaches fourth grade at Aberdeen (N.C.) Middle School in Aberdeen, was in Washington with her husband to visit relatives and Mrs. Clark.

Mrs. Clark graduated from Indiana State Teachers College in 1930. After teaching elementary school for two years, she quit to raise her children. She and Ed Clark were married until his death in 1973. She resumed teaching in 1953, the year Mrs. Crain entered her class as a first-grader.

After she retired from teaching public school in 1976 at age 65, she taught seven years at a mission school in Arizona.

"Every year I tell my students about her and how she inspired me to be a teacher," says Mrs. Crain.

Carol's Responsibility Chart

Responsibility is doing what needs to be done, when it needs to be done, whether you feel like or not, and without having to be told over and over to do it.

Carol copied or adapted this "responsibility chart" quotation from *Reader's Digest* or some other publication, and used it in her classroom.

She believed in teaching responsibility. Students had to hand in work. Student infractions resulted in their copying the responsibility chart various numbers of times.

After she retired, Carol and I (her husband) were sometimes eating in restaurants when former students approached her and said that of the things they remembered from her classes, the responsibility chart stood out. One former student said she was teaching the quotation to her children. Another of Carol's former students stood in a restaurant parking lot and quoted the responsibility chart to Carol.

A former student told her about his Army experience and the responsibility chart. He had served at least one foreign tour of duty. When in charge of physical training for a group of soldiers, he presented the responsibility chart quotation and required them to quote it back to him during exercise sessions. One soldier asked, "Where'd you get that saying?"

"From my fourth-grade teacher in North Carolina," he responded.

Carol loved decorative sweaters, usually bought from used-clothing consignment shops. Her Envelope Hugs reflected her love for people and words.

Sending Envelope Hugs

Carol E. Crain enjoyed sending "Envelope Hugs" to friends and to some people she did not know. After retiring from teaching fourth grade at Hoffman Elementary School in Hoffman, North Carolina, she sent increasing numbers of envelope hugs. Carol described her efforts below in an article written on May 1, 2007:

I send handwritten, hand-created notes, often including songs and poems I've written and quotations I've collected. What I send depends on the situation a person is going through—whether he or she has cancer, has lost a child, is going through a divorce, whatever the need is.

I don't type my notes and letters or use e-mail. I write my letters, my "Envelope Hugs," in longhand. I think this means more in a day of e-mail and junk mail.

I have many kinds of cards and stationery, and I hand-make some cards using magazine pictures. I've been doing this off and on since I was in college in South Carolina. Most of my friends and relatives lived in Pennsylvania, and I began sending cards and letters.

My husband and I married a year after we graduated from college, and each taught school for a year. He left for a year in Vietnam only a few months after we married. I wrote him many letters during his army service (almost two years). And I kept in contact with some college friends and my relatives.

I've continued contact with many people who have specific needs. Sometimes I read in the newspaper about someone going through difficulties, and I follow up on that. It just depends on what I feel led to do in reaching out to a person.

After I went through malignant melanoma cancer in 1985, I've tended to notice people who were going through any type of cancer. I know how they feel when they're told they have cancer. When you've been through something like that, you belong to a fraternity or sorority you never wanted to join, but since you belong, there's some good that can come out of it since you understand.

I put lots of different things in envelopes. It depends on how well I know the person, as to what I enclose. If I don't know a person, I'll tell them, "Even though I don't know you personally, when I heard about your situation, I wanted to share with you, and I hope the things I've sent to you will be a blessing to your life."

I go through the songs and poems I've written, especially those written since about 1974, and I think about which one or ones might be most helpful to them. One thing I've had to settle is that it doesn't matter if I hear back from people. I know that the fact that I felt the Lord putting it on my heart to write to them in the first place means there was a reason for it. If I never know what they got from what I sent and how it ministered to them, it's okay. Sometimes I think the fact that I don't know them is what ministers most to them because they realize I took time to write, even though I don't personally know them.

Sometimes I send several different letters to the same person, but often it's a one-time thing. It just depends.

Of the people whom I don't know, I hear from a few. Once in a while, someone will write a note to me, saying thank you for sending the things I sent. But sometimes they're so involved in what they're going through that I don't think anything about not hearing from them.

Sometimes I read an obituary, cut it out of the newspaper, and then wait several weeks before I follow up. I may follow up by writing the next day, or I may wait several months, because I think that after everything gets back to the day-to-day grind for people that it may mean more to them when someone reaches out to them by writing—after the visits, the phone calls and the mail have long ago quit coming.

I often call the church where the funeral was held or a funeral home to get a person's address. If it's local, I look in our phone directory.

I call my creations "Envelope Hugs." I did a workshop on "Fun with Snail Mail: Creating Envelope Hugs" for a few ladies who came to my home, and I have conducted larger workshops for church ladies' groups. I like to invite about four ladies to my home and show them how to reach out to others using their own personalities and contacts. Whether it's a mother who stays home with her baby or an elderly person who can't get out much, anyone can send a letter of encouragement, an envelope hug, to people who need ministry.

Not all my cards are handmade. But sometimes I clip a picture from a magazine and write a quote with a Sharpie pen on that magazine page. I collect quotes. I put lots of little things in an envelope along with a card or letter—songs, poems. I don't spend a lot of time keeping track of everything I send to people. I do try to track which songs and poems I send, so I won't send one twice. I keep a date book listing people and the dates I've written those people.

I received a touching response from an elderly man who had been married over sixty years when his wife died. He approached me at church after I'd sent him something almost every day for several weeks after his wife died. He told me how much my cards had meant to him. I sent cards with pictures of dogs, boats, lighthouses, nature scenes, etc.

"I have them standing up in each room, and when I go from one room to the other, and I look at your notecards, they're like company for me," he said tearfully.

I thought that was a very meaningful way to describe what it means for a lot of people who go through their mail and see a personal piece of correspondence in the middle of all kinds of bills, pleas for money, and junk mail. I wrote a lady who was going through cancer, and she said that she kept my envelope hugs in a box, and when she felt especially down, she'd take my letters out and reread them. She said they ministered to her, again, and even in a different way.

Sometimes the Lord will impress me with something specific to share in an envelope—maybe a picture or something to say. Then later I find out why that particular item meant something to the person receiving the letter.

One time I wrote a lady I didn't know very well who was going through cancer. I'd met her in the downtown store she owned. I felt I should cut out some paper dolls from a magazine. They were only little childlike dolls. I cut out the dresses and the dolls and included them in an envelope with other items. I wrote, "I used to play with paper dolls when I was a child. Did you ever have any paper dolls?"

One day when she was especially down, she went to the post office and received that piece of mail. She said she opened my letter, saw the paper dolls, and experienced such a warm feeling as she thought back about her childhood, when she had a collection of paper dolls and her mother designed clothes for those dolls. She said her mother would draw the clothes, cut them out, and give them to her to color for her dolls.

That was a very good memory she had, and she knew I had no way of knowing. She said she felt God gave her that special memory of her mother through my sending those paper dolls. It made her feel close to her mother while she was going through cancer treatments.

We became good friends. One night she called, and I sang some of my songs for about forty-five minutes to her over the telephone. She said it was like hearing a lullaby that gave her peace before her first chemotherapy treatment the next day. She later died from cancer.

Another time, a lady's army-officer husband spent two tours in the Middle East and returned safely to the United States. Not long after his second return, he died in a head-on collision near their home. I didn't know her personally but knew of her in our community.

I sent her and her three young children mail almost every day for months. I sent things of age-level interest to the children and sent her songs and poems and prayers the Lord would lay on my heart for her. I handwrote all those. I received only one or two postcards from her during the months I was writing but never wondered why she didn't respond more. I knew she was probably completely overwhelmed with her husband's death and being the single parent of three young children.

One day I came home after an especially hard day of teaching. This was probably a year and a half after I'd begun sending envelopes to this young widow. I'd tapered off from sending letters after several months, but I was still sending something once in a while. When I pulled into my driveway, there was a beautiful shopping bag, like a gift bag, on my porch.

What's that there for? I wondered. *It's not my birthday.*

The lady I'd written to had given me a whole shopping bag of very expensive stationery and notecards. She'd gone to a shop downtown and probably spent over $200. She handwrote a little card, saying she wanted me to know how much all the things that I'd sent to her and her children had meant to her.

It seemed as though the Lord was giving me encouragement to go on and do this for other people. I still use some of the stationery she gave me, and I think of her and the encouragement I felt.

I met another lady, Sharon, years ago at a Bible study. She had been through a divorce and had two small children. She lives in a distant state, but that friendship has spanned almost thirty years. We still send notes, letters, and packages, and we also call each other.

I kept in contact with my first-grade teacher, Mrs. Esther Clark, until her death a few years ago. She was an inspiration to me, and I never forgot her. I now correspond with her daughter.

One of my fifth-grade students (1998) liked to write poetry. She moved away mid-year of the year I taught her. We've stayed in touch, and I encourage her in her writing.

Another young lady—I read her essay about how she felt when her dog had to be put to sleep—began writing after I wrote her. She's now married and has children. We've stayed in contact.

I've sometimes written to famous people, but I mostly write everyday people.

I often include cards with quotes inside bills I pay. I never know when God may use a devotional quote to encourage someone who is going through a hard time and need to know God cares about them.

Sometimes people respond long after I've written them. Often their responses come on days I need something.

There's a young lady at the gas station. I broke my ankle in 2004, and the healing process had been long. This young lady, if she had no inside customer, would come out and pump my gas for me. I sent her an envelope hug.

I have to have peace that I follow up on contacts when I need to. Some contact information may sit on my desk for a while.

Years ago, a local man died when he accidentally drove his small truck in front of a speeding train. He was on the way to buy materials to build a playhouse for his grandchildren. I didn't know the man or his wife, but when I read about the accident in the newspaper, I felt I should send something.

My note stayed for several weeks on my desk, until one night about 10 o'clock. I was turning out the lights in my office and felt I should fix an envelope and send it the next day. I spent about an hour preparing that letter and things I included in the envelope. In the letter, I apologized to the deceased man's wife for waiting so long to reach out.

She soon called and said the letter came exactly when it was supposed to because the envelope arrived on the day of their wedding anniversary.

When a young fellow teacher died in his early forties, I sent his wife and four children envelopes. One devotional book I sent arrived . on her husband's birthday. She said that meant a lot. I hadn't known about his birthday. The Lord knows exactly what these people need. I try to stay open about that.

What do I put in my letters and envelopes?

Sometimes I put childish things, whimsical things, artwork. I collect calendars with pictures of animals, barns, and a variety of all kinds of things. I try to make these very individual and out of the ordinary.

I wrote one couple whose young daughter was accidentally run over and killed at a family reunion. I noticed in the obituary that the daughter was the age of the children I taught at that time, and the Lord put that family on my mind many times. I'd sit in church some Sundays and write out prayers for them, which I'd send them. The father called me, and the mother and their remaining daughter wrote to me. The father told me how much all the things I sent had meant. I still sometimes send them things.

I feel like the Lord puts certain people on my heart because he knows whom it would touch and mean something to. I can't cut out all the obituaries in the newspaper every day, seven days a week.

It's not always the obituaries.

I read about a murder in another state and sent an envelope to the reporter who wrote the story about the murder. I wrote to the family of the deceased, also.

I want to listen to the Holy Spirit, and stay open to letting the Lord use me to minister to hurting people and to use the talent and the gift he's given me in writing songs and poems and make these creative things to help people feel ministered to when they're in lots of pain.

Many of my poems and songs came from working out the healing of the memories of my childhood.

When I was diagnosed with cancer, my minister said to me,

"You've written a lot of things to minister to people who needed inner healing for hurtful experiences in their lives. And now maybe you'll write things to minister to people who are going through serious illnesses."

I remember looking at him and saying, "Well, maybe. I don't know." And the very next day, the Lord began to give me one song and one poem after another.

How do they come to me?

Songs come to me in the way that people think of their favorite Christmas carols. You can hear it in your mind. You can hum it. That's how they come to me. The music usually comes at the same time the words do if it's a song. I've pulled the car over and written words on a paper bag or anything when they come. Then I sing my new songs into a tape recorder.

The poems come sometimes when I'm reading the Bible or a devotional book or any book. I write down quotes from things I read or hear. I have a lot of journals. I'll write something someone said and then what that quote makes me think about. I'll write, "Helen Keller said …" or, "Abraham Lincoln said …" and share them in a letter. I have hundreds of quotes.

Writing has always been a very cathartic way to receive healing from the Lord for me. I write as I listen to sermons. I write as I watch a movie on TV. I write while reading devotional books and magazines. I've always related to writing. I think a lot of people don't realize how they could be used in this way in their own personalities and creative abilities to reach out to people they'll never meet.

I suppose people hesitate to reach out to others because sometimes no words seem adequate. But human words are all we have, and I hope God can use things I share in envelopes to ease pain.

Sometimes people don't know what to say, so they don't say

anything, and a needy person thinks, *I thought they cared more than that.*

Other times people don't know what to say, so they say ridiculous things, which don't help at all. They mean well but say inappropriate things. But at other times, God gives people words that are exactly what someone needs at a particular time. I've spoken to people at times rather than wait to write to them.

I have several notes in progress. I don't write ten or fifteen every day. I am now working on a note to a friend who has experienced divorce after forty years of marriage. She's alone now. I've sent her all sorts of little messages telling her I care about her. And I'm always looking for little interesting things, little cartoons, little magazine pictures, all kinds of things to put in an envelope to convey that the Lord loves her and cares about the things she's going through.

We never know when people may be suicidal, and the Lord may use an encounter with us to let a despondent person know how special they are and that the Lord cares about them.

Some may have never thought about being used by God in this way, this way of writing and reaching out, this way of sending envelope hugs. Especially people who can't get out of their homes very much can reach out by letters.

Some may look at others and think, *Oh, they have more gifts than I do. They're up in front of people in my church.* But this is something shy people can do. Retired people can do. Shut-ins can do. People in nursing homes, those who are able to write something at all can do this. Mothers who are home with babies can write while their youngsters take naps.

I sometimes used to get up in the middle of the night or write from 4:00 a.m. to 6:00 a.m., before I went to work. But now that I'm retired, I devote many hours to writing personal letters.

Someone may think, *Well, that's just something special that God is doing through her, but God couldn't use me like that.* I think God can use many people.

Some fear the rejection of not hearing back from people. But you need to feel that if you don't hear from anyone you send mail to, it's okay. If you start keeping track, saying, "Four weeks ago, I wrote Sally, and I never heard anything. And I sent thirty pieces of mail to so-and-so over the last year because they went through thus-and-thus, and I never heard." If you start keep track like that, you will lose the meaning of what this is all about. You don't do it so you'll get a reply.

Finding that shopping bag on my porch was like a thirty-page letter to me. It was like the Lord saying, "See. I am encouraging you to keep on keeping on with this. See how much it does mean to people." And it wasn't about how much money that young mother spent on the stationery she bought for me. It was about what she felt impressed to do.

There are no two letters or envelopes I've done that are identical. There are no two people alike. There could be five people going through cancer, but you don't make five envelope hugs that are all alike. Each person is different and individually special to God.

I like to take time to think of each person I'm writing to. I want to create something just for that specific person. I don't send e-mail, though I don't criticize those who do. Many of us associate e-mails with stock items we copy and send, maybe send to fifty people with one click of a computer key.

In a world becoming more and more obsessed with technology, my envelope hugs ministry reaches out in a personal way. I print because my printing is much more readable than my longhand writing. I prefer printing over typing letters because of the personal character of handwriting.

Some say to me, "I bet you enjoy scrapbooking," and I say, "No, I really don't." My envelope hugs are a form of scrapbooking; I'm just mailing the pages out to people. I may take a piece of paper and glue a word or pictures from magazines. Then I may write about what that word makes me think of. You can be creative.

Peggy, one of my friends, sends creative envelope hugs to me. I'll send her a letter about childhood memories, and often, when she returns a "hug," she'll take the same picture I sent and write a note about what the picture made her think of. Or she'll take a quote from one of my letters and write about why that quote ministered to her. I recently opened one of her letters before I went to my beautician. She'd written about not allowing people to steal the joy from our lives. I read that letter to my beautician. I feel Peggy's letter ministered to her. I wrote Peggy and told her that she ministered to the lady who styles my hair. I sent Peggy about twelve kinds of notecards so she can use them to write other people. Sometimes I include blank notecards and say to the person I'm writing, "Maybe you'd like to send a card to someone today."

When I write, I picture the person receiving my letter and looking at each little thing I've included in the envelope. I have all different sizes of envelopes. Often I'll put a smaller envelope inside a larger one and write on the smaller, "Open tomorrow," or, "Open on Sunday," or, "Put in your pocketbook and open whenever." When I feel impressed to be creative in this way, I believe it's a beautiful manner in which God is showing the person receiving the note that he is ministering to them in a very special way, a way that is all their own.

Another friend tended to respond by writing formally but has become more creative in her responses over the years as I set an example of finding joy in writing. I feel her newfound creative expressions have eased some of the melancholy in her life.

My notes, letters, and handmade cards don't appear mass-produced. I even put a little bow around a set of quotes I recently copied from a devotional book. I wrap some notes in brightly colored cloths before tucking them inside envelopes.

Years ago I read an article in *Home Life* magazine about a Christian couple whose daughter and son lived away from home and shared an apartment in the town where they attended college. While the brother was away from the apartment, an intruder broke in and killed his sister.

I wrote the grieving mother and shared heartfelt sympathy. She and I have been writing ever since. At the time of the trial for their daughter's murderer, I had a dachshund, and so did she. When she and her husband traveled around Easter time to attend the trial, they took their dachshund with them. In one of her notes, she mentioned the name of the hotel where they were to stay during that trial.

I prepared a care package to send to the hotel so it would be waiting for them when they arrived. I included all sorts of Easter things, such as Easter candy, a stuffed Easter bunny to decorate their hotel room, dog biscuits, and a journal for her husband and one for her son, who was twenty-one years old.

Before I closed the envelope, I felt I should send a letter from my dog to her dog. I didn't want to seem ridiculous or frivolous in light of the serious ordeal they faced. Yet the idea of writing a dog-to-dog letter wouldn't leave me. I had stationery with dachshunds printed about the paper's border. So I wrote, "To Ellie Kay from Dudley." I wrote two or three pages from our dog, Dudley.

When my friend received the package, she went to a drugstore, bought a card with dachshunds on it, and wrote a return letter from her dog. She included lines such as, "Mom and Dad talk about how the jury is going to be chosen. They're going to have to see the person who did this to their daughter," and, "They both pet me a lot."

I felt the Lord inspired me to write in a manner—a seemingly childish way—that helped my friend get out her feelings in a way she was able to deal with, through the imaginary words of her dog.

Through the years I've sent little dachshund things and my songs and poems to her. And I've also mailed notes to the father and the brother. We've enjoyed years of staying in touch, and I met her through responding to a magazine article about her tragedy.

A day hardly goes by that new contacts don't come across my path. Here is one of my favorite quotes by an unknown author: "It was only a kindly word / And a word that was lightly spoken / Yet not in vain / For it stilled the pain / Of a heart that was nearly broken."

That's what I want my envelope hugs to do. I want them to still the pain of hurting people.

A Summary of Carol's Homegoing

Steve Crain

In December 2012, a probable blood clot formed in and moved from Carol's leg, bursting in her lungs, and causing pulmonary hypertension (PT). "Most people don't make it to the hospital in your condition," Dr. Michael Pritchett told Carol. He became Carol's pulmonologist and was affiliated with FirstHealth Moore Regional Hospital in Pinehurst, North Carolina. Since that day, Carol battled PT. Carol's body had low pressure, but her lungs maintained high blood pressure because hundreds of tiny blood clots from that original burst lodged in her lungs.

We were living in Southern Pines, North Carolina, where we had lived since 1989. I had worked at Gulistan Carpet, a carpet manufacturer, since 1989. Gulistan declared bankruptcy, and I ended my employment there on January 10, 2013, right after that blood clot damaged Carol. I was two months away from age sixty-six at that time.

On Tuesday, October 17, 2017, Carol entered FirstHealth Hospital with congestive heart failure. She had wanted to stay in Southern Pines because of her doctors, but she felt during that hospital stay that the Lord impressed her to tell me, "Let's move back to Greenville, South Carolina." Our older daughter, Janelle Smith and husband, Terry, live in Taylors, part of metro Greenville.

I said, "We're about too old to move."

Realtor Chuck Hust guided us on buying a Taylors' house on December 15, 2017, in Greenville. We moved to Taylors on January 10, 2018. The Rev. Steve and Mrs. Sherry Sturm of Greenville helped us much. The Rev. Jerry and Mrs. Jan Brown of Bethlehem, Georgia, helped us unpack.

Carol was hospitalized in Greer from November 3 to 14, before transferring to North Greenville Hospital, LTACH (long-term acute-care hospital). She stayed at LTACH from November 14 to December 13. She was at home during Christmas and New Year's Day 2019.

At 10:30 p.m., Wednesday, January 2, 2019, Carol said, "I need to go to the hospital." An ambulance took her to Greer Memorial Hospital. One blood pressure reading for her showed 71/27.

On Thursday, Dr. Armin Meyer, Carol's pulmonologist after our move, told Carol he had done all he could do. He recommended hospice care. Carol was being kept alive by meds that helped raise her BP while fluid was taken from her body by diuretics. Carol also had chronic lymphedema in her legs for years. She reached an impasse.

On Sunday, January 6, Carol seemed depressed. Charles Fleming (a first cousin of mine), his wife (Sandra), and Joy (their daughter) visited the hospital room. Two of their sons, Pastor Travis and Mark, visited, too, along with Travis's wife, Jenna. Travis, visiting from their home in Gallatin, Tennessee, prayed for Carol.

On Monday, January 7, Dr. Meyer took Carol off all sustaining medicines, and she was transported to Hospice House of the Carolina Foothills in Landrum, South Carolina. "We give only comfort medications here," the admitting nurse said.

During her hospice stay, Carol received "squirts of morphine derivative" as needed for discomfort. "Don't leave me here in this place by myself," Carol said.

"I won't," I said. I slept on a couch near Carol.

"I tried so hard," Carol said at one point.

"Yes, you did," I said. "But your heart is wearing out."

On Tuesday, January 8, our daughter Janelle Smith and her husband, Terry, visited. On Wednesday, January 9, Janelle and Terry returned in the afternoon. Carol took off her engagement and wedding rings and handed them to Janelle. Tears flowed, but Carol shed no tears. I think the "distancing" I'd read about was taking place inside Carol, and she was weak and tired.

That night I sat beside Carol and cried and told her how much I would miss her. She did not cry but seemed peaceful as she held my hand. I prayed for her and watched her sleep for a while.

On Thursday, January 10 (our one year anniversary of moving to Taylors), visitors came: Donna Tidwell, a longtime friend; Jan and Jerry Brown; Sherry Sturm; Connie Rogers, a teacher friend of Carol's and her husband, Don Rogers from Pinehurst; Pastor Bill Montgomery (age eighty-eight); and Janelle.

Carol lapsed into sleep by nightfall. I called Janet Rice, Carol's longtime friend. Janet talked to Carol by cell phone. Carol didn't respond, but I think she heard Janet.

On Friday, January 11, Carol seemed unconscious. Sherry Sturm visited and left. Pastor Jerry and Jan Brown returned, and at 12:10 p. m., we three sat around Carol's bed. Jan suggested singing hymns. We sang three songs, and Jerry said, "I don't think she's breathing.

The young nurse came. She put her stethoscope on Carol chest, and after a long silence, the nurse said, "There's no heartbeat." Carol had slipped out peacefully around 12:20. The nurse asked us to sit in a family room. Soon, a representative from the funeral home arrived to move Carol's body to Wood Mortuary in Greer, South Carolina, my hometown.

We held Carol's funeral service at noon, Wednesday, January 16, 2019, at Wood Mortuary's chapel. Pastor Jerry Brown led the service. Pastor Steve Sturm spoke. Four of Carol's longtime friends spoke: Janet Rice, Sherry Sturm, Jan Brown, and Donna Tidwell. Pam and Bobby Mason and Robert Duckett provided music. I also gave a tribute to Carol.

Carol often sang a song she wrote that is based on St. Paul's statement, "To be absent from the body is to be present with the Lord." Sometimes, in my mind, I hear Carol's voice singing that song. Waves of grief frequently hit me. I was in a grocery store and saw a kind of coconut cake Carol liked. Tears came. We had grown even closer as Carol depended on me during the last year of her life. I'm glad I was able to deliver her into our Father's hands.

Obituary for Carol E. Crain

(published in *The Greenville News*, January 14, 2019)

Carol Ellen Williamson Crain, 71, of Taylors, S.C., died on January 11, 2019.

Born in Oakland, California., she grew up in Washington, Pennsylvania, as a daughter of Betty Lee Day and the late Edward Williamson. She was a retired teacher and a member of Sandhills Assembly of God, Southern Pines, N.C.

Also surviving are her husband, Larry Steve Crain of the home, and two daughters: Janelle Lee Smith (Terry) of Taylors, S.C., and Suzanne Crain Miller (Chad) of Raleigh, N.C.

Mrs. Crain affirmed that she "accepted Christ as her Savior" when she was four and a half years old at a "Vacation Bible School held at Broad St. Baptist Church in Washington, PA." A 1969 Bob Jones Univ. graduate, she taught at Gateway Elementary School in Travelers Rest, S.C., before moving from Greenville, S.C., in 1988 to N.C. She last taught school at Hoffman Elementary, Richmond County, N.C. In recent years, she led inspirational book discussions and mailed letters to many, calling her letters "Envelope Hugs." She and her husband moved from Southern Pines, N.C., to Taylors, S.C. in January 2018. After a six-year battle with pulmonary hypertension, she died peacefully at Hospice House of the Carolina Foothills, Landrum, S.C.

Funeral services will be held 12:00 p.m., Wednesday, January 16, 2019 at the Wood Mortuary (Greer, SC), conducted by Rev. Jerry Brown and Rev. Steven Sturm. Burial will follow in Hillcrest Memory Gardens.

Visitation will be held 6:00-8:00 p.m. Tuesday, January 15, 2019 at The Wood Mortuary, Greer, S.C.

The family is at the home. In lieu of flowers, memorials are suggested for Assemblies of God World Missions, 1445 N Boonville Ave., Springfield, MO 65802, or Hospice of the Carolina Foothills, P.O. Box 336, Forest City, NC 28043.

A young Carol poses with a puppy.

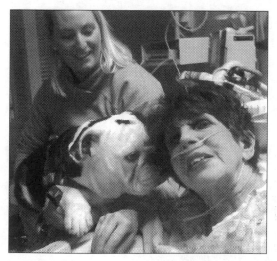

This December 2018 picture of my late wife, Carol (right) with a therapy dog and its owner is the last photo I made of her. (Steve Crain)

Places Carol Worked as a Teacher

Alexander Elementary, fifth grade, Greenville, South Carolina (1969–1970); Cone Elementary, Fitzsimmons Army Hospital, Aurora, Colorado, teaching GED preparatory classes for soldiers; Fairview Elementary, Greer, South Carolina; Fountain Inn Elementary, Greenville, South Carolina; Greenville County School District Office; Tanglewood Middle, Greenville, South Carolina; Westcliffe Elementary, Greenville, South Carolina; Parker High School, Greenville, South Carolina; Adult Education Department, North Plainfield, New Jersey; Gateway Elementary, Travelers Rest, North Carolina; Woodland Baptist Christian School, Winston-Salem, North Carolina; West End Elementary, West End, North Carolina; Aberdeen Elementary, Aberdeen, North Carolina; Hoffman Elementary, Hoffman, North Carolina.

Index

About the Author

Carol E. Crain, author of No Clouds Tomorrow, reached out to many people with her songs, poems, and Envelope Hugs. Her works touched lives. No Clouds Tomorrow contains a large number of Carol's inspiring writings.

Born in 1947 in Oakland, California, as part of the post-World War II baby boom, Carol met her father only once. Raised in Washington, Pennsylvania by a single mother, she spent much time with her maternal grandparents. She became a Christian at age four-and-a-half at a Vacation Bible School at Broad Street Baptist Church in Washington. In her first-grade classroom, she was the only child from divorced parents; her first-grade teacher, Mrs. Esther Clark, inspired Carol to become an elementary school teacher.

At Bob Jones University in Greenville, S.C., she met Larry Steve Crain, an art education major. They graduated in 1969 and married in 1970. Carol taught at public elementary schools in S.C., gave birth to two daughters, and lived for almost 30 years in N.C. while her husband worked in carpet manufacturing. Carol retired after teaching at Hoffman Elementary, a N.C. public school. The Crains moved back to Greenville County, S.C., one year before Carol died from pulmonary hypertension in 2019.

Carol's passion for teaching and for her Christian faith guided her outreach and led her into many positive encounters throughout her lifetime. Her songs and poems reach out to fellow travelers who suffer from depression and struggle with memories of hurtful relationships or life experiences. In No Clouds Tomorrow, Carol's article about Envelope Hugs will inspire those who desire, through letters and greeting cards, to influence and comfort others.

Printed in the United States
by Baker & Taylor Publisher Services